EXPERIENCE THE MOST FREEING JOURNEY OF YOUR LIFE
BY UNLEASHING . . .

YOUR ARTIST WITHIN

TOM BIRD

YOUR ARTIST WITHIN

TOM BIRD

SOJOURN, INC.

Requests for such permission should be addressed to:
Sojourn, Inc.
P.O. Box 4306
Sedona, Arizona 86340
www.ambassu.com

Bird, Thomas J.
        The Artist Within

Cover Design: Manjari Graphics
Layout: J. L. Saloff
Fonts used: Capitals, Century Schoolbook, President, Staccato

ISBN: 0-9707258-9-2

ABOUT THE
AUTHOR

Tom Bird was only twenty-six years old when he dropped to his knees and made his urgent plea.

"If you show me how to connect with the artist that is so desperately trying to get out of me, God, I will always make time to share this secret with others," he stated.

Two nights later, Bird was awakened from a sound sleep with the solution he had requested.

A publicist with the big league's Pittsburgh Pirates at the time, but an aspiring author at heart, he immediately put the plan that was shared with him into play. His efforts met with instant results. Within two weeks, he landed the services of the publishing industry's most renowned literary agent, who sold the rights to his first book to the third largest publisher in

"The last quarter of a century of my life has been pretty constantly and faithfully devoted to the study of the human race – that is to say, the study of myself, for in the individual person I am the entire human race compacted together. I have found that there is no ingredient of the race which I do not possess in either a small way or a large way."

MARK TWAIN

the world only a few weeks later.

True to his word, Bird began offering his secrets shortly thereafter. Over the last two decades, Bird has made more than 2500 teaching appearances at over 100 of the country's top universities and colleges, including: Duke University, the College of William and Mary, the University of Texas, Ohio State University, the University of Nebraska, New York State University, and Old Dominion University. During that period of time, he has shown tens of thousands how to connect with and then direct the artist within us all.

Besides that, Tom has penned 13 books, and his byline has appeared in dozens of publications. His books include: *Willie Stargell* (Harper & Row, 1984); *KnucklesBALLS* (Freundlich Books, 1986), coauthored with big league Hall of Famer Phil Niekro; *Hawk* (Zondervan, 1996), written with future Hall of Famer Andre Dawson; *POWs of WWII: Forgotten Men Tell Their Stories* (Praeger, 1990); *Fifty-Two Weeks or Less to the Completion of Your First Book* (Sojourn, 1990); and *Literary Law* (Sojourn, 1986). He has also contributed to such distinguished magazines and newspapers as *Parade, USA Today, The American Banker, The Pittsburgh Post Gazette,* and *Sail.* In addition, he has also recreated the experience of his revolutionary workshops in an interactive computer program for writers, *The Author's Den.*

Tom's continued success has led him and his work to be featured in *USA Today, The New York Times, The Los Angeles Times, The Philadelphia Inquirer, The Chicago Sun-Times,* and over 100 other publications. His work has also been fea-

"Art is a collaboration between God and the artist, and the less the artist does the better."
ANDRE GIDE

tured on most of the nation's top news and inter-
view programs including "The David Letterman
Show," "The Tonight Show," "CBS Morning
News," "The Today Show," "The Charlie Rose
Show," "CBC," and "The 700 Club."

And now, just for you, Tom has taken all of
the secrets behind how he and his students have
connected with their Artists Within (AW) and
shared them in this book.

"Be bold – and mighty forces will come to your aid."
BASIL KING

ACKNOWLEDGMENTS

Many hearts, souls, and minds contributed to the successful completion and publication of this extraordinary book. Thank you to Jamie Saloff for her refinement and formatting of my material; Manjari Graphics for the cover; Evelyn Still for copyediting; Tammy Kelley, Tom Puetz, and Bill Lucas for their encouragement; to my many students; and most of all, to God, for the reason, the time, the energy, the resources, the message, and the way.

"To feel themselves in the presence of true greatness many men find it necessary only to be alone."

TOM MASSON

To learn more about Tom and
his innovative programs,
or to potentially sponsor one of his
retreats or classes in your city or town,
feel free to either call his office
at 928-203-0265 or check out
his website at:

www.YourArtistWithin.com

DEDICATION

To Tammy:

Thank you. You are the keeper of the key to a certain part of me that I couldn't have gotten to without you.

* * *

For what we did share, what we do share, and what we will always share.

Love always,

Tom

XIV

TABLE OF CONTENTS

TABLE OF CONTENTS

TABLE OF CONTENTS

INTRODUCTION

Before the age of two, life couldn't have been better. It was a game to be played and enjoyed. You may have had so-called imaginary friends who loved you unconditionally. Every possibility was real. There were no hidden emotions or disguised agendas. You spoke and acted as you felt and were appreciated for doing so. If you were sad, you cried. If you were mad, you yelled, and if something was funny, you laughed. Life was easy, honest, and expressive. What more could you ask for?

But then the ax fell. Even though it may have gradually infiltrated your life, a point came when the line was drawn, and all that was previously acceptable was no longer okay. It was no longer all right to openly express your emotions and feelings – no matter how correct they may

"Teach your children that they will never be judged, that they need not worry about always getting it right, and that they do not have to change anything, or 'get better,' to be seen as perfect and beautiful in the eyes of God."
NEALE DONALD WALSCH
Communion with God

have been. No. Rules and regulations were put upon you. You were expected to fall in line and to become a productive, law-abiding member of society — just as your parents had done and your grandparents and so on and so on and so on down the legacy of your heritage.

Your parents, with the unrelenting pressure of society upon them, were pushing you in the direction of the all-encompassing, strength-through-numbers pack to which they belonged. All of a sudden you were expected to talk a certain way, to walk a specific way, and to dress or carry yourself appropriately. No longer were you allowed to tell anyone how mean and terribly ugly he or she was, even if it were the truth. No. Your parents, out of a need to protect you, were going to share everything they knew about how to remain safe — which is what they equated with happiness. The result? You would end up becoming just as at peace, fulfilled, and as satisfied with your life as they were with theirs.

Unfortunately, in their desire to love you just as deeply as they could, they forgot that you already possessed a level of joy, oneness, and happiness that they forgot was even possible. For they, like you, had the essence of truly being loved and living snatched from them by your grandparents, who had this same lifeblood cleansed from their consciousness by their parents. This deflating tradition had been in place for hundreds if not thousands of years. And then it was your turn to bow to it.

No matter how tight a relationship existed between you and Your Artist Within (AW). No matter how natural this relationship happened to be. No matter how diligently you may have

"Little Lamb, who made thee? Dost thou know who made thee?"

WILLIAM BLAKE

2

fought back during the time casually referred to as 'the terrible twos,' you were destined to lose. There were just too many of those who loved us and cared about what happed to us and who just did not know that something better existed outside of what they were offering us; you were just so small and they were so big; and all of society was behind their loving but inappropriate guidance.

So, in the broad, sweeping contradiction that was becoming your life, lying through omission of truth and true feelings was acceptable, and even the use of drugs was okay as well, as long as they tamed your bucking bronco and got you to color inside the lines and got you to stop talking out so darn much.

After the initial and painful break with your AW was complete, you were conditioned to march to the beats of the lives others expected you to live. No longer were you cute, lovable, and loved unconditionally. Some day soon you would be stepping out of the nest, and you had to be prepared for it. Who and what you had been before would no longer be good enough.

Then our collective fates were transferred into the caring but overworked hearts of those within the educational arena, which had its own unique sets of rewards that it relied upon to try and help us 'fit.'

If we adhered to and embraced the orders that were placed upon us, we were rewarded. If we followed the rules really well and said what we were expected to say and answered only when spoken to, we were applauded.

Of course, these accolades came at a cost. That cost, of course, was the last thing the indi-

"Mistakes are the portals of discovery."

JAMES JOYCE

3

viduals within the system wanted to extract from us, that, of course, being the loss of our true selves and our innate purposes, and the ostracization of our AWs.

Sure, after or during this time, there might have been a temporary fling or two when you revolted against the system and during which time you may have even innocently stumbled upon your real self. You may have flunked out of college because you partied too much. You may have gotten suspended in high school a few times. But somewhere along the way, usually after the pain of getting ostracized from the tribe became too great, you fell back into the fold. This all happened because the conditioned fears of your past pulled you back. These were the same exact fears that pulled your parents and your parent's parents back into place as well.

And you soon found yourself in the same depressing dilemma – paying taxes that were unconstitutional, living where you didn't want to live, doing what you didn't want to do with your life, and passing along or preparing to pass along this legacy to your children and the next generation.

What you were taught to fear the most, which forced you to sell out your AW, even came to fruition. Most of these fears, if not all, were just legacies blindly passed on to you and openly accepted by you – simply because you didn't know better.

Oddly, these unnatural fears struck at the very heart of what our democracy was supposedly designed to nurture – freedom in all forms and the ability to live your life as you choose. Yes, what I am saying is that what you fear most is

"It is hard to fight an enemy who has outposts in your head."
SALLY KEMPTON

4

your own ability to succeed to the highest level of your forgiving heart and its infinite potential. However, to succeed to that most sought after of levels spills you outside the control of the tribe, and we have been inappropriately conditioned to believe that to cross that line equals danger and almost certain death.

That myth about those who valiantly cross that line, the real heroes of democracy, is so blatantly and inappropriately reinforced in our society that these rare, wonderful examples of what we all can be are openly chastised by all forms of media. And the memories and collective fates of those who stepped over the line are never far behind as well.

Christ, Abraham Lincoln, John F. Kennedy, and Martin Luther King, Jr. What happened to each of them? And you don't believe their collective demises had an effect on the shunning of your own AW? Think again. These all-conquering impressions, when combined with the conditioning you acquired as a youth and continue to receive, have made all of the difference. Most of it may all be buried deeply within the catacombs of your psyche, but it's there.

To find the proof of what I speak, you need to look no deeper than the results or lack of results of your own life. It was initially the conditioning of your youth, as well as the follow-up you have and still receive, that has caused you to arrive where it is that you are with your life – which is a good and bad thing.

Maybe you are not where your soul and heart, through your AW, calls you to be – so that could be seen as bad. But it is that same bad – your forsaking of your real self – that could have

"He must forget the things he does not wish to remember and remember only the things he wishes to retain."
BAIRD T. SPALDING
Life and Teaching of the Masters of the Far East

5

"In the depth of winter, I finally learned that within me there lay an invincible summer."
ALBERT CAMUS

possibly caused enough pain to make you consider trading all you are for all you feel called to be. And so you picked up this book.

Congratulations! It's time to release that AW-you who has been clawing at the door for possibly a decade. It's time to turn the page and let he or she out and live like you've never lived before.

———————— ❦ ————————

Our deepest fear is not that we are inadequate.
Our deepest fear is that we are
Powerful beyond measure.
It is our Light, not our
Darkness, that most frightens us.
We ask ourselves, Who am I to be brilliant,
Gorgeous, talented, fabulous?
Actually, who are you not to be?
You are a child of God.
Your playing small does not serve the World.
There is nothing enlightening about
Shrinking so that other people
Won't feel unsure around you.
We were born to make manifest the
Glory of God that is within us.
It is not just in some of us; it is in everyone.
As we let our own Light shine,
We unconsciously give other people
Permission to do the same.
As we are liberated from our own fear,
Our presence automatically
Liberates others.

Nelson Mandela*

*As quoted by Marianne Williamson in her book, *Reflections on the Principles of a Course in Miracles*, Harper Collins, ©1992

CHAPTER ONE: THE ARTIST WITHIN US ALL

AND THE PURPOSE OF OUR LIVES

Your connection with your art was first evidenced in you at an early age. Maybe you were the child who never took lessons and yet loved to sing. Possibly you were the youngster for whom playing 'doctor' was so much more of a passion than it was for your playmates.

No matter what it was, the result of your magnetic draw, which I refer to as a person's art, need not even have had anything to do with any of the visual and performing arts, such as painting, sculpting, writing, acting, or dancing.

The art to which I am referring can fall into any number of fields from medicine to law to counseling and to an unlimited collection of other activities. An artist in this regard is best defined as "one whose work shows great creativity or skill; one who is adept at an activity; or

"Do what you can, with what you have, with where you are."
THEODORE ROOSVELT

one who creates imaginative works of aesthetic value." (*The American Heritage College Dictionary* – Third Edition)

A good example of this can be found in the life of my recently deceased close friend and big league Hall of Famer Willie Stargell. Willie was obsessed with the swatting of stones with sticks as a child. Eventually that obsession was transferred to bats and balls, and the remainder of his glorious story speaks for itself.

Willie discovered his art form and the AW in himself at an early age. Eventually, when a gun-bearing bigot in Plainview, Texas, threatened to kill Willie if he played in a minor league game one evening, Stargell quickly discovered how important and obsessive this lifelong draw really was to him. That evening, he was faced with the most important decision of his young years, and he came to the realization that living a life without living his art was not worth living.

"I believe that catalysts are presented to us in various stages throughout our lives," claimed Stargell, in his 1984 autobiography that I coauthored with him. "They force us to either go forward, change our rhythm, or retreat. I believe that fear sometimes forces us to make our most monumental decisions. Such was the case with me in Plainview. I was at the crossroads of my life. Should I face the situation bravely and overlook the threat, or succumb to the fear I felt and drift slowly away from the game I loved?

"After hours of deliberation, I felt the power. I had only one alternative, to keep playing. If I was going to lose my life, at least I would lose it doing what I loved doing."

Willie's situation with his AW was both

"There is surely a piece of divinity in us, something that was before the elements."
THOMAS BROWNE

10

unique and typical. His obsessive draw, which is alive in all of us when young, was not unusual. What was out of the ordinary was that his family, no matter how many windows he shattered, encouraged him to follow with all his heart his unique, but yet undefined, calling. The contagious enthusiasm and joy that poured forth from Willie as he played the game he loved affected not only those directly around him but eventually tens of millions of viewers who watched that era's most popular athlete perform.

Because of the unconditional nurturing that Willie received as a child, the life or death decision concerning our AWs, which usually hits us when we are least prepared and ready for it around the age of 24 months, was reserved for when the future slugger was better ready to make his decision at the age of 19.

For the average human being, the age of two is when our well-meaning society, filtering itself down through our parents, forces boundaries, rules, and regulations into our lives. Strength is found in numbers, and there is no greater security than being a living, breathing, active, and participating member of our societal tribe.

By becoming a participating member of the same tribe our parents, families, neighbors, and region belong to, we, despite how valiantly we fight back during our terrible twos, are asked to sacrifice our art and our God-given selves. For most of us, there is no other option available.

So dramatic is this loss of self and this force ostracizing the divine connection we have with our AWs that most people then fall prey to decades of supposed safe lives of quiet desperation. Only if they are lucky, do their lives even-

"The very purpose of existence is to reconcile the glowing opinion we hold of ourselves with the appalling things that other people think about us."
QUENTIN CRISP

11

tually erupt in what is referred to as a midlife crisis, which is unfortunately usually squelched after a bit of what others see as their 'acting out.'

Even a much smaller number are fortunate enough to make it through this second adolescence and come out on the other side with their AWs and life purposes completely intact. In her award-winning book entitled *Awakening at Midlife*, my student, Kathleen Brehony detailed how a proactive embrace of what is commonly referred to as a midlife crisis can make all the difference in the world. Good examples of how a loving acceptance of this time and situation can lead to a true, overwhelming happiness and sense of peace, unlike any other in a person's life.

When Tammy and I met it was a 'love-at-first-sight' attraction. She is a marvelously loving, creative, intelligent, and caring person. Yet the status of her hodgepodge life at the time did very little to reflect her true potential.

While we were living together, we would oftentimes spend 10-12 hours just talking. In our initial conversations, much that she questioned me about had to do with how it was that I had found my purpose and how it felt once I did. For Tammy had never had any experience resembling anything that I shared. During that time as well, I questioned her often and in great depth about what it was that she really wanted to do. Then finally one night, the reply I sought surfaced in a few simple words. "All I ever wanted to do was to work with children."

A few months later, we parted, after Tammy began calling for space. Three months later, we reconnected even more strongly than we had connected in the first place. But by this time,

"Through surrender, spiritual energy comes into the world."
ECKHART TOLLE
The Power of Now

Tammy's life had changed drastically. She had faced her necessary life or death decision, and she had reacted proactively by giving up everything to relocate to a primitive Indian village at the base of the Grand Canyon to teach children.

The metamorphosis she experienced was immense. All of the symptoms of a lost and frustrating lifestyle were gone. She was focused, committed, and directing all of her fine energy into her art.

When I questioned her about her dramatic life shift, she replied with ease and all of the confidence in the world.

"I've always been a teacher," she replied.

Tammy and her AW had again become one. Her life and her viewpoint of it were again perfect.

Most people's Artists Within are buried under many years, if not decades, of convenient excuses which they use to squelch the pleas of their art. In most cases, these same people replace the positive addiction of their AW-self with earthbound, societally-fed, negative obsessions, designed to detract from them their true callings.

These same people eventually pass away, having lived not a wasted life, but yet one unfulfilled by their AW's true and fullest purpose.

However, you are not destined for that fate. You are different. No matter what your reason may be for choosing a different route by reading this book, this work – serving as your compass – will lead you home to you, your art, and to your unique connection with your AW.

Age is not a factor that either negatively or positively affects your decision to take this most

"I will work in my own way, according to the light that is in me."
LYDIA MARIA CHILD

13

*"Conformity is the jailer of free-
dom and the enemy of growth."*
JOHN F. KENNEDY

important of all steps. Some like Stargell, Tiger Woods, or child prodigies such as Mozart, Stevie Wonder, or Michael Jackson were either encouraged to embrace and ride the ride of their AWs or were somehow defiantly strong enough to survive the push to live an unnatural life.

Others travel much farther down the roads of their lives. They then rediscover their AWs, and from that point forward they leave behind their divine imprint on life.

Age isn't a deterrent in reconnecting with your AW. Neither is your gender, social or economic background, education, religious beliefs, color, creed, or sexual preference. The importance of your connection with your AW transcends all of the factors we are usually led to believe are important.

At this juncture in your life you don't even need to have any idea what it is that you believe your art to be. Your actual connection may be buried that deep beneath prior learning. In fact, the overdeveloped societal side of yourself, which seeks to keep you within the boundaries of the tribe, may have created some politically correct purposes in your life. You may sense these to be your art. However, no matter how hard you may have worked to become proficient at these activities, they still will not hold for you the same degree of self-satisfaction and peace as your art.

There are many time- and money-consuming psychotherapies that deal directly with this age-old, life-zapping dilemma. Frontal lobotomies are also still available as well. However, all that you truly need to make the most life-giving transition of your life is this book and the time needed to read and play your way through it.

CHAPTER TWO: HOW TO USE THIS BOOK 2

I am the fifth of five children and the youngest in my family by nine years. Thus, by the time I came along, my parents had grown wise enough to realize the true value of every day and every life. So, they encouraged me to go wherever it was that my art was leading me. Yet, even with their encouragement, pursuing my AW's call to writing was still not a natural fit for a resident of a hardworking, blue-collar town such as Erie, Pennsylvania.

At about the age of fourteen I still had a bucketfull of doubts. Just so 'different' was my call when compared to that of my more conservative friends. So, late one evening, as I lay on my parents' side lawn staring up at the stars, I finally asked the questions of God that had been haunting me for years.

"Lord, make me an instrument of Your Peace. Where there is hatred let me sow love; where there is injury, pardon; where there is doubt, faith; where there is despair, hope; where there is darkness, light; and where there is sadness, joy."
ST. FRANCIS OF ASSISI

"Why is it that I want to write?" I questioned.

The answer, which I could kinesthetically feel vibrating through every fiber of my body, came back to me in an instant.

"You want to write because that is your way of conveying all of the beauty you see in life so that others may begin to see it as well," was what It said. Shortly after, the obsession to write, to communicate what was in my heart since childhood, finally began to make sense.

Little did I realize at the time how substantial the acceptance of this fact would be. Not only did it lead me to my purpose and my career, but writing eventually also led me to the system, the way, the art form that would enable me to lead so many others to their AWs and their purposes. For even though writing is only one of tens of thousands of art forms that one could choose from, it is an activity that almost everyone has performed. Thus, whether authorship is what you want to do or not, the art can be used to enable you to reconnect with your AW, your art form, and your Divine purpose. To best allow the art of writing to permanently return you to the Artist Within, it is important that you consider using the following suggestions with the exercises you will be asked to complete. That said, please keep in mind the following directives:

> **First**, make sure to find yourself a quiet, comfortable space in which you will be uninterrupted.

> **Second**, make sure that you have a pen. Lineless paper, the larger the better, will also be necessary. Blank sheets have been provided in this book for many of the

"All of Jesus' healings were on the basis of removing the mental cause."

BAIRD T. SPALDING
Life and Teaching of the Masters of the Far East

exercises. In some cases, though, you may have to go outside this book.

➤ **Third**, before beginning an exercise, insure that your arms and legs are uncrossed and remain uncrossed at all times.

➤ **Fourth**, breathe in and out through your nose only.

➤ **Fifth**, close your eyes, and keep them closed until you are ready to write.

➤ **Sixth**, if at any time you feel tense, for any reason at all, breathe in deeply through your nose and then blow out all of your tension through your mouth before going back to smoothly inhaling and exhaling through your nose only.

➤ **Seventh**, if at any time you feel as if you have run out of something to say or the speed of your writing has dropped drastically, close your eyes, breathe out any tension, and reconnect with the image that caused you to express through your writing in the first place.

➤ **Eighth**, write as fast as you can at all times, not taking any time during the writing process to edit or read over your work.

➤ **Ninth**, let your words arrange themselves however they choose on your paper.

➤ **Tenth**, you may choose to employ the use

"If at first the idea is not absurd, then there is no hope for it."
ALBERT EINSTEIN

17

"If I repent of anything, it is very likely to be my good behavior."
HENRY DAVID THOREAU

of a tape player to record in advance and then play back for yourself the relaxation and visualization steps that follow for each of the exercises.

➢ **Eleventh**, sit back, relax, and let your almighty Artist Within lead you and your writing wherever you are destined to go.

————————⟨Ⓥ⟩————————

CHAPTER THREE: HOW RELEASING YOUR ARTIST WITHIN

WILL CHANGE YOUR LIFE

Have you ever had any of the following happen to you?

➤ Have you ever been performing an activity that you found to be creative and enjoyable and it just seemed to pour uncontrollably out of you?

➤ Have the results of this activity ever carried with it a degree of intelligence or insight that you had a difficult time accepting as your own?

➤ While taking a long drive in a car, have ideas ever flooded your mind?

➤ Have you ever awakened in the middle of the night with a desire to express something or to write something down?

"Regret for the things we did can be tempered by time; it is regret for the things we did not do that is inconsolable."
SYDNEY J. HARRIS

"Tis God gives skill, but not without men's hands. He could not make Antonio Stradivarius' violin without Antonio."

STRADIVARIUS

> ➤ When you have gone away on a relaxing vacation have you ever gotten the strange urge to enter into this activity again?

> ➤ Have you ever daydreamed so deeply of this activity that you could actually feel yourself doing it?

> ➤ Has an activity ever been so closely tied to you that it seemed to refuse to let go of you?

If you answered 'yes' to any of the above, you are already very familiar with the connection to your AW, your art, and your purpose, which forms the basis of this book.

In fact, the truth is that you've probably been in direct communion with your invigorating, all-powerful, all-seeing, all-knowing art, which attaches to something way beyond yourself, thousands of times in your life.

You know the one I'm referring to – the connection that caused you to feel as if you could have danced all night and did; when you knocked down strike after strike in bowling, nearly rolling that perfect game; when, while playing golf, the hole seemed as big as a trashcan lid; when difficult tasks at work or at home were accomplished in record times and with amazing ease, as if someone or something was working through you and guiding you to their successful completion.

You've been there – thousands of times – when you feel something wildly exciting, yet strangely calming and comfortable, and widely intelligent, talented, yet beyond our human conception. This feeling can express itself through playing a game, a piano, any other instrument, a chosen profession, or merely through talking.

Others Who Have Experienced It

Amazing accomplishments, rates of completion, and qualities of productivity take place while in the midst of one's art. This sensational connection is also not limited to any one endeavor or activity and has been expressed in every aspect of life from the arts to athletics to business to personal endeavors and interests of all kinds.

In the world of music, for example, Mozart felt and welcomed his art, which allowed him to brilliantly express his music at an age when most other composers were still playing with blocks.

Beethoven felt it, recognized it, and gave in to it, which is why he was able to compose his most masterly symphony at a ripe old age, teetering at death's door, after he had gone stone deaf.

In the business arena, modern icons such as media magnate Ted Turner, the czar of the ever-expanding computer industry Bill Gates, and many others as well, rode its calling to success and set their respective fields afire.

In his book *My Life and the Beautiful Game*, Pele', the great soccer player, described the state in this fashion:

"I felt a strange calmness," wrote Pele', . . .

"In heaven an angel is nobody in particular."
GEORGE BERNARD SHAW

21

"a kind of euphoria. I felt I could run all day without tiring, that I could dribble through any of their team or all of them, that I could almost pass through them physically. I felt I could not be hurt. It was a strange feeling and one I had not felt before. Perhaps it was merely confidence, but I have felt confident many times without that strange feeling of invincibility."

In the world of writing, this connection is prevalent and available.

While one with his connection, Jack Kerouac wrote his finest works in only a few sleepless days.

Ernest Hemingway felt so excited and stimulated that he wrote while standing up. Thomas Wolfe did the same and, since he was so tall, actually did his writing on the top of an icebox.

Samuel Beckett, the award-winning playwright, wrote his cornerstone of modern drama, *Waiting for Godot*, in a mere few months while in this state.

Singer/songwriter Harry Chapin wrote his 1970s blockbuster hit *Taxi* in less than thirty minutes while standing in a subway.

You have been there yourself, have you not, when a passionate activity literally took over and took control?

An individual student of mine, while in this state and working on the completion of her first book, wrote over 25,000 words, the equivalent of 85 double-spaced pages, in one day. Another completed over 17,000 words in the same period of time.

In both cases, their works, upon being edited, were found to be nearly without flaw.

I spoke to the former of the two students

"Its visits, like those of angels, short and far between."
ROBERT BLAIR

22

immediately after she had completed her day of work.

"You must be tired," I probed.

"Well," she replied with pretty much the same spark in her voice in which she had started the day, "I could go out dancing. I'm not too tired to go out to dinner or to attend a movie. Frankly, I am not physically, mentally, or emotionally tired at all. I'm just tired of writing."

"My dear, I don't care what they do, so long as they don't do it in the street and frighten the horses."
MRS. PATRICK CAMPBELL

WHAT IS IT?

As it has been since Jackie Robinson's breaking of the color barrier, the arena of modern, big-name athletics has been a trendsetter. Its titling of this connection was innovative as well. Its christening of this connection as the 'zone' spread rapidly across the globe. Others have chosen to employ other terms.

"Now this creative power I think is the Holy Ghost," clarifies Brenda Ueland, author of *If You Want to Write.* "My theology may not be very accurate but that is how I think of it. I know that William Blake called this creative power the Imagination, and he said that it was from God. He, if anyone, ought to know, for he was one of the greatest poets and artists that ever lived.

"Now Blake thought that this creative power should be kept alive in all people for all of their lives and so do I. Why? Because it is life itself. It is the Spirit. In fact it is the only important thing about us. The rest of us is legs and stomach, materialistic cravings and fears."

Depending on your chosen point of reference,

whether it be religious, psychological, scientific, artistic, or romantic, what I am referring to as your AW has been described in several ways ranging from the Holy Spirit, to the Muse, to the Greater Consciousness, to the Subconscious, to the Right Brain. No matter what terminology you may have used in the past though – it all describes the same entity – your AW.

This AW connection is also oftentimes personified in the form of some entity. It also has far-reaching capabilities and is willing to meet you through what I refer to as your CCM, or Creative-Connected Mind, while behind a paint brush, a chisel, a keyboard, a desk, a podium, on a stage or dance floor, or wherever it is you choose.

As already mentioned, you know your AW, who comes through your CCM. Your AW is the one that floods your CCM with ideas and inspirations associated with your art when you are on a relaxing beach or mountain vacation, or when you are on a long drive by yourself in a car. It is the AW that awakens you through your CCM in the middle of the night, and pours out so rapidly at times that you feel out of control, maybe even pleasurably out of control.

Both your AW and CCM, the bearers of your art, have been awaiting this time for what seems forever. Now is the time to consciously meet your AW, face-to-face, pen-to-pen, heart-to-heart.

"It is not necessary to seek God because God is already the essence of who you are. To connect with God, simply remove all judgments and thoughts that do not bless you and others."

PAUL FERRINI
Reflections of the Christ Mind

24

Meeting Your Artist Within

Step 1. Take a moment to close your eyes and to relieve any tension that you may be feeling by taking deep breaths through your nose and blowing them out through your mouth. Do this until you feel stress free and worry free. This will not only relax your body, but what I refer to as your Logical Critical Mind or LCM, setting free any potential internal distractions. Follow all the other preparatory instructions in the How To Use This Book section as well.

Step 2. Once this has been accomplished, it will be easy for you to go back in your mind to the time when you first recognized, for whatever reason, you were being drawn to perform a specific creative activity. Let this time, this place, and all that goes with it come to life in your mind. Relive it in great detail by asking yourself the following questions:

How old were you at the time?

Where were you?

What was it that you were wearing?

Was anyone else there?

What time of year was it?

What time of day?

"The true God, the mighty God, is the God of ideas."
ALFRED de VIGNY

Was it an incident, a person, whatever, that caused you to want to be so creative?

What was it that you were doing?

What was it that you remember most about this incident?

What was it that you felt strongest about?

Step 3. Following this exercise, open your eyes, pick up your pen, and allow whatever it is that you feel to be released on the blank page. Remember to let the words flow, to write as fast as you can, to breathe away any tension and/or resistance, and to abstain from reading over or editing your material at this time.

As you can see from the previous exercise, you were born with the ability to connect to your AW. Then who or what has stopped you from living through this connection? *You.*

Yes, the truth is there are many outside factors that attempt to influence your free will, but you are the only one who can keep your dreams from becoming a reality. If outside influences were as dominant as we make them, then persons such as Maya Angelou, who worked her way out of the ghetto to become one of the most respected writers in modern history, or Frank McCourt, who rose from a severely dysfunctional upbringing to become a bestselling author, and hundreds of thousands who have walked just as challenging a route, would have never ended up where they did.

No matter what the cost or what barriers stand between them and their dreams, some people just choose to follow their inner voice, that magical, all-knowing connection they hear calling them forward – their AWs – while others respond to another voice, that logical/critical calling of outside influences telling them to "Stand still," "Don't move," or even worse, "Turn tail and run!"

But why is it that anyone would allow this essential connection to be severed? The answer is simple. They just didn't know any better, and they listened to those who didn't know any better as well.

"I did not write. God wrote it. I merely did His dictation."
HARRIET BEECHER STOWE

FEARS

Before we dig any deeper though, let's venture a little further into the fears of success, which, as I mentioned at the beginning of this book, we have all been plagued by in one form or another.

In general, these fears have caused you to worry that if you become a success your friends, spouse, and family, with whom your relationships may have been conditional (as opposed to unconditional), would no longer like or love you, or vice versa. You could also fear the reprisals that you may have experienced on previous occasions.

Which of the following fears do you resonate with? How do you know if you resonate with one or not? The stronger your reaction to any of the following statements, even when that reaction comes in the form of a desire to ignore, the more tied to the potential realization of it in your life you are. Fears of success can be divided into two distinct categories: *Fears of Change* and *Fears of Loss*.

*'Let me assert my firm belief
hat the only thing we have to
ear is fear itself."*
FRANKLIN D. ROOSEVELT

EXAMPLES OF FEARS OF SUCCESS

FEARS OF CHANGE

> *"If I succeed, I will be expected to continue to do so, and I'm not sure that I will be able to follow through."*

30

"Hey, I've been living the same style of life for as long as I can remember. I've had the same job for years. I've lived in the same house and the same town for what seems like forever. My life may not be everything I want it to be, but no one can guarantee me that it wouldn't be a heck of a lot worse were I to risk it in going after what it is that I think I really want."

"Successful people are always on the go. They're always doing something, touring here or there. They have wealth and esteem. Everybody knows them, and I'm just not cut out for all that stuff."

"People will know more about me than I am comfortable with them knowing."

"I'll be seen as being crazy."

"I will look like a fool."

"The world likes the little guy. It's the guy with all the money and fame that it dislikes. Assassinations are reserved for those with power and fame. No one has ever heard of a nobody being attacked for who they were."

"Who knows who I would have to sleep with or lie to to get there. I'm just not willing to sell myself so short in that way."

"The illusion of Failure is necessary in order to experience the exhilaration of Success."
NEALE DONALD WALSCH
Communion With God

FEARS OF LOSS

"Those closest to me just won't understand me anymore, and there's nothing I value more

31

than their company, attention, and affection."

"If I end up where it is that I want to go, for the first time in my life I will have something in my life that I will love and, thus, I will fear losing it."

"My life may be far from perfect, but at least I am in control of it. If I were to succeed, there is no doubt that I would lose the structure I need to live, exist, and that is just not acceptable."

"I will be hounded by all sorts of responsibilities. I will no longer have my own time, my own life."

"I will be overtaken by my love for what it is I do, and I won't be able to fulfill my obligations to those around me. As a result, they will eventually end up disliking me or possibly even leaving me."

"I would have to leave those I love to do what I want to do."

"The failure of outer things to satisfy leads the soul to seek the power within."
BAIRD T. SPALDING
Life and Teaching of the Masters of the Far East

EXAMPLES OF FEARS OF FAILURE

Fears of success are only one of the two major strands of fears. The other less powerful one deals with Fears of Failure. Since we are typically exposed to this form of fear at a very young age, Fears of Failure initially cause us to reject our AW. It is, of course, only after you break through these barriers that you are awarded the opportunity to experience your more major fears, those of success.

Fears of Failure fall primarily into one category.

FEARS OF LACK

"No one would be interested in what I'd have to say or do anyway."

"Anything that I would try on my own wouldn't work."

"No matter what I do I always wind up screwing up."

"I have a difficult time believing that I deserve anything good in my life."

"I'm not smart enough."

"I don't have enough money."

"I'm not attractive enough."

"I'm not brave enough."

"I'm not dedicated enough."

"I'm not serious enough."

"I don't have good luck."

"I haven't paid my dues."

"I'm not talented enough."

"I'm too old."

"I'm too young."

"Obstacles are those frightful things you see when you take your eyes off your goal."
HENRY FORD

33

"I don't have anything to say."

"Who would want to hear what I have to say anyway?"

THE MAN OR WOMAN IN THE MIRROR:

THE GOOD NEWS IS YOU CAN REVERSE IT

It is up to you to decide what it is that you will do with your life. Now is the time to take back control and move swiftly and joyfully in the direction of your dreams and aspirations. Just like a light socket responds only to a certain size bulb, you won't be able to find your way home unless you begin seeing yourself as your AW sees you. That's step one, a step of self-reconnection.

The following exercise, which works like a salve for the removal of the above fears, is designed to help you do just that. Compared to other forms of cleansing, this exercise is short in duration but possibly great in intensity. For it, you will need a mirror. You are encouraged to stay with this exercise for however many sessions are necessary. If you need to employ more paper than has been included, do so. Just ensure it is of the lineless variety. Stay with it until you can look yourself in the eye and feel nothing at all in response to the following statements. Then, and only then, will the noose of the previous fears have been loosened enough for you to move on to the next phase.

"The only service a friend can really render is to keep up your courage by holding up to you a mirror in which you can see a noble image of yourself."
GEORGE BERNARD SHAW

34

Step 1. Position yourself in front of a mirror.

Step 2. Take time to close your eyes, clear your mind, and relax.

Step 3. Then, open your eyes and, using the mirror, look yourself directly in the eye and repeat the first statement, allowing any and all thoughts or feelings, to spill out onto your paper. After you have done that, repeat the statement again and allow whatever it is that arises to spill out onto the paper again. Do this over and over and over again, until, as mentioned, you can look yourself in the eye, repeat the statement, and feel nothing. Then move on to the next statement and do the same thing. Once you have completed your work with statement number two, then follow the same exact steps with the third statement, and the fourth, and then the fifth and final one. Do not move on to the next chapter until you can look at yourself in the eye and repeat any of the five statements and feel absolutely nothing.

"Until you look in the mirror and see your own beliefs reflected there, you will be using every brother or sister in your experience as a mirror to show you what you believe about yourself."

PAUL FERRINI
Reflections of the Christ Mind

FIVE STATEMENTS

1. *"Life is my best teacher; it provides me with all that I need to know."*

2. *"My mind is an endless storehouse of ideas and inspirations."*

"Teach them that failure is a fiction."
NEALE DONALD WALSCH
Communion with God

3. *"I do best what I like to do most."*

4. *"What I like to do most brings me the personal success that I desire."*

5. *"What I like to do most affords me all the opportunities I desire to live my life as I choose."*

Chapter Four: Your Journal

4

Since you have now officially begun communing with your AW, it will be appropriate for you to keep track of your efforts and growth. For you to do so, I have included journal pages at the back of the book. This journal will become a source of accountability for you as you grow rapidly toward where your AW is taking you.

As you will notice, at the top of each of the ninety pages, room has been left for you to number each of the days of your progress. They have deliberately been left blank so you can individually adjust this journal to use with your own art.

For example, if your art calls you to work on a series of short pieces or to maneuver through the series of exercises in this book, each of which only takes a few days, you can individually number each sequence. Conversely, if you will even-

"I always say, keep a diary and someday it'll keep you."
MAE WEST

tually be working on a lengthier project, such as a book – which could take up to 90 days then you can consecutively number the pages. Either way, no matter what your AW calls you to do, these journal pages have been specifically designed to aid you in releasing and directing Your Artist Within.

When using this journal, be completely accountable and honest with yourself. If you had a challenging day and, as a result, you did not successfully complete your goal, say so. Remember, the entire process that you have entered into is about expressing your feelings and about releasing your AW. That means on all levels. So always be honest and true to yourself.

Whether you choose to informally share what you have written with others is another matter. My suggestion is to avoid doing so at all costs. My reasoning for offering such a suggestion has to do with the fragile and thus vulnerable state in which you will find yourself as you strip off the veneer to reach the AW within you.

You will also notice that space has been left for you to list whatever reinforcements you have offered yourself and what nice things you have done for yourself each day. Paying special attention to these two areas is a must. For, in releasing our AW, we are embracing a whole other lifestyle, one built around love and doing what we love. So, it is important that you become accountable for your AW's showing of that love first with you. Because then and only then will you be able to share that same love with others.

Flip to the back of the book, and take a look at the journal pages. Then fill out the first page with what you have done or will do for today.

"The only true happiness comes from squandering ourselves for a purpose."
WILLIAM COOPER

Time I scheduled to meet with my AW:

Time we actually met:

Our goal for today:

What we actually accomplished today:

Reinforcement I planned to offer myself for a job well done:

Reinforcement that I gave myself:

Other observations and notes:

My goal for my next session:

When we will meet again:

What I will use to reinforce my positive actions after the next session:

Time I scheduled to meet with my AW: 5 a.m.

Time we actually met: 5 a.m.

Our goal for today: Write 3,000 words

What we actually accomplished today: 3,343 words

Reinforcement I planned to offer myself for a job well done: A glass of wine after dinner

Reinforcement that I gave myself: That fine glass of wine

Other observations and notes: I still cannot believe how this whole process just grabs me and leads me along. It's taking me to a place I always wanted to go, but I was afraid to try. Now I feel more comfortable with each session as I see how so much of this is out of my hands. Amen.

My goal for my next session: 3,100 words

When we will meet again: Tomorrow at 5 a.m. again

What I will use to reinforce my positive actions after the next session: That well-deserved glass of wine again

Chapter Five:
LCM Versus CCM
And the Three "Rs" of Writing

5

As daunting as the fears you just faced may have been, there is a simpler, faster, less expensive way beyond long-term psychotherapy, and/or a frontal lobotomy, to deal with them and to keep them from affecting your life so dramatically.

Even though the solution I am about to offer has roots going as far back in history as the Yin and Yang and its connection with the I Ching, its most recent version was popularized by Roger W. Sperry and his students at the California Institute of Technology in the 50s and 60s.

Sperry's hypothesis eventually became tabbed as the split brain theory. At the essence of Sperry's work is the fact that humans actually have two independently functioning brains as opposed to two lobes. Sperry's proving of his the-

"We are traditionally rather proud of ourselves for having slipped creative work in there in between the domestic chores and obligations. I'm not sure we deserve such big A-pluses for that."

TONI MORRISON

ory revolutionized the way people viewed how they thought, expressed, and lived life.

Shortly after the release of Sperry's work, bestselling books began appearing on the shelves, such as Betty Edward's *Drawing On the Right Side of the Brain* (Tarcher, 1978) and Gabrielle Rico's *Writing the Natural Way* (Tarcher, 1983), which confirmed that we no longer had to suffer deprivation and frustration to pursue the arts of drawing and writing. In fact, all we had to do was know how to self-induce an AW-based state, and to keep from rejecting that state after it arrived.

What I am about to share with you is an evolution of Sperry's discovery and an extension of follow-up theories. However, it is built upon my own discoveries, some of which fall outside the lines of information gathered by Sperry and others. So, I felt that it would be best to rename the two major components that we will be discussing.

I have chosen to christen what is commonly referred to as the logical mind or left brain, as the Logical/Critical Mind or LCM. As far as the component routinely called the right or creative brain, I have chosen to go with the Connected/Creative Mind or CCM. As you can see from the following, these two separate sides of yourself are opposites.

"Light breaks where no sun shines; Where no sea runs, the waters of the heart push in their tides."

DYLAN THOMAS

52

The Characteristics of Your
LCM Versus Your CCM

Your LCM:	Your CCM:
Purpose: Avoid Pain	Purpose: Expression
Thinks, Evaluates, Criticizes	Feels
Conditional	Unconditional
Limited Capabilities	Unlimited Capabilities
Falsely Dominant	Innately Dominant
Short-Term Memory	Long-Term Memory
Sleeps	Never Sleeps

LCM

The LCM has been a tremendous asset in your life. It has led you to graduate from school, to the acquisition of degrees, to landing jobs and keeping them, to paying your bills, and stopping at stop signs – just to mention a few of the tens of thousands of privileges it has bestowed upon you.

However, as much of an asset as it has been, it has led you away from living up to your fullest potential by interfering with and, in some cases, completely shutting down your connection with your Artist Within. This, of course, was not its intention, for the LCM, just like every other part of you, simply wanted you to experience a happy and productive life.

However, it was trained, conditioned to keep you away from your AW. Most of this damage, as mentioned earlier, happened around or before the age of two. This was the period in your life when your CCM and, thus, your AW connection, ruled your life. Society changed all of that. As a result, you have spent the better part of your emotional/spiritual life since then trying to recover your real self, your AW.

To help you better understand how to best deal with your LCM in this recovery back to the real you, I have listed and expounded upon the characteristics of your Logical/Critical Mind below.

YOUR LCM'S PURPOSE: TO AVOID PAIN

When you were born, your LCM was like a

"We must cultivate our garden."
VOLTAIRE

blank hard drive. Nothing had been written upon it. All that it learned came as a result of its tie to your five senses, upon which it eventually became dependent.

During the first two years of your life, it learned all about sensations and feelings. It craved peace and happiness and learned to seek out whatever situations, people, activities, or stimuli that offered it that. It also learned to avoid that which caused it, and you, pain.

So painful and consistent were the rules and regulations placed upon you during your childhood that your LCM, in an attempt to protect you, took on the role of society in rejecting your CCM and its connection with your AW.

Thus, since that time, your LCM, which was forced away from its role of supporting your AW and CCM, took over. Since then, in response to the pain it was taught to associate with your Artist Within, your LCM has done whatever it could do to keep you away from your AW. As a result, it has consistently steered you away from following the calls of your AW. To best make my point in this regard, I ask you to take a few minutes to complete the following exercise.

"The conscious mind must seek and want the spirit in order to learn the power of the spirit."
BAIRD T. SPALDING
Life and Teaching of the Masters of the Far East

WAY BACK WHEN

Step 1. For the following exercise you will need to be alone in a quiet space and be in possession of a pen.

Step 2. Take time to close your eyes, clear your mind, and relax.

Step 3. Allow your AW to take you back to the

time when you first realized that following its calling, for whatever reason and in whatever way, shape, or form, was something your Ultimate Source was calling you to do. Where were you at the time? Were you alone? If not, who was there with you? What was it that you were doing at the time? How old were you? Do you recall any sights and/or sounds that were part of your experience at the time? Where was it that your AW was calling you to go? What was it that you saw yourself doing or what was it that you wanted to do? Take a few more deep breaths to release any tension and allow yourself to feel as if you were back at that time and place. Breathe in the experience and then open your eyes, pick up your pen, and write however it is that you feel. Keep writing and feeling for a minimum of five minutes nonstop, making sure not to stop and read your material. Just allow how it is that you feel to flow out unadulterated.

"Creative minds always have been known to survive any kind of bad training."
ANNA FREUD

From the above exercise, you can get an idea of how long it's been that your LCM has been keeping you away from the callings of your AW. You may also have caught a glimpse of the tactics it may have used to keep you away from it. Now, take a few minutes and perform the next exercise. Allot a minimum of five minutes for each of the two sequences.

INTERRUPTIONS, INTERRUPTIONS, INTERRUPTIONS

Step 1. Once again, find yourself alone and in a quiet place with your pen.

Step 2. Close your eyes, clear your mind, and relax.

Step 3. Allow your AW to go to the last time it was that you were actually following the guidance of your AW. What was it that you were doing? How were you feeling? Where were you? How old were you? And why was it that you stopped doing whatever it was that you were doing? Be honest. Feel your feelings. Allow yourself to go back to that time to recall. Breathe in the experience and then open your eyes and allow your feelings to spill out onto your paper.

Step 4. After you have done that, close your eyes and assume your relaxed position again.

Step 5. This time allow your AW to take you back to a time when you looked criti-

"Remove the illusions, lift the veils, and you will rest in the heart. Rest in the heart, and God will abide with you."
PAUL FERRINI
Reflections of the Christ Mind

59

"Not to be able to stop thinking is a dreadful addiction, but we don't realize this because almost everyone is suffering from it, so it is considered normal."
ECKHART TOLLE
The Power of Now

cally upon the connection you had with your AW. Why were you feeling as you were? What was it that you were feeling? Open your eyes and describe why you were feeling as you were.

The purpose of the above exercises was to demonstrate for you the role your LCM, as protector, has taken in response to your AW. Your LCM has done whatever it could to keep you from connecting with your AW.

1. It has tried its darnedest to keep you from connecting with your AW.

2. It has interrupted you when you have connected with your AW.

3. And it may have inappropriately judged, and thus put down or even destroyed, whatever it was that you and your AW produced together.

Your LCM is not a bad brain. In fact, it is quite the opposite. As mentioned, it has led you to good and great accomplishments in your life. It has also done a tremendous job of keeping you out of harm's way. Unfortunately, because of the inappropriate training that was laid upon it, it has lumped your connecting with your AW in with life dangers, such as sticking your head in a fire or drowning.

All of this comes as the result of your LCM's role as protector, which causes it to lead you away from anything painful and encourages it to lead you toward whatever it is that it deems pleasurable.

"The one great thing man must learn is to get forever through and out of the psychic or mind forces and express directly from God, for all psychic forces are created wholly by man and they are likely to mislead."
BAIRD T. SPALDING
Life and Teaching of the Masters of the Far East

THE LCM THINKS/EVALUATES/ANALYZES AND CRITICIZES

To best perform its task, it is essential for the LCM 1) to evaluate every situation, 2) to think about or to ponder every circumstance before any step is taken, and 3) to criticize actions, situations, and people that it has been conditioned to deem as dangerous. Since it has been given the role of your protector, your LCM believes that this sequence of events is absolutely necessary to insure your safety. And your LCM will remain steadfast in whatever decision its analytical capabilities reach until proven otherwise. That is what this entire book is designed to do: to prove it otherwise.

THE LCM IS CONDITIONAL

Another byproduct of the LCM's role as protector is that it is conditional. In other words, the LCM needs to know in advance the outcomes of an activity before it decides whether to participate or not.

So, it is going to do its best to stop you from communing with your AW, in any way, shape, or form, if all that it knows of your experience with art comes from painful experiences of your past.

Your LCM will also do its best to keep you from wasting time with your AW, if it believes you to be in any way inadequate to complete an artistic task.

"He gets away from God, and instead of letting God express through him and the perfection that God sees for him, he goes and expresses in his own way and brings forth imperfectly the thing which should be perfectly wrought or manifest."
BAIRD T. SPALDING;
Life and Teaching of the Masters of the Far East

64

The LCM Has Limited Capabilities

As mentioned, your LCM was like an empty hard drive when you were born. It knew nothing, and all that it eventually learned came as a result of its exposure to your five senses.

In fact, it probably was not designed to fit the protector role. It took the role of protector only after being exposed to the extreme attack launched against your CCM. It was at that point your LCM not only became your dominant brain but the purpose of your life switched from one of expression to one of survival.

Your LCM Is Falsely Dominant

Innately, your LCM was designed to support the inspirations of the CCM. However, it had no other choice than to take on the role of protector. However, its control actually became one of false dominance.

Your LCM Houses Your Short-Term Memory

We have both a Short-Term Memory (STM), which is a temporary holding bin of information that stores stuff for a short period of time, and a Long-Term Memory (LTM), which holds onto facts, figures, thoughts, feelings, and experiences forever. Your STM is part of your LCM.

"When we were little we had no difficulty sounding the way we felt; thus, most little children speak and write with real voice."

PETER ELBOW
Writing With Power

65

YOUR LCM SLEEPS

Because of its limited capabilities and its STM, your LCM was not designed to be a leader, let alone a full-time one. Thus, it sleeps when you go to sleep or, when you just relax, it nods off.

YOUR CCM'S SOLE PURPOSE IS TO EXPRESS

While your LCM's acquired purpose is one of survival, to avoid pain and to lead you to what it instead associates with pleasure, your CCM's sole purpose is to express the beauty, insight, and inspiration of your AW.

Whether you realize it or not, you are a very significant part of the giant puzzle that we refer to as life. Thus you are responsible for bringing a lot more to this plane than just paying off another mortgage or raising another dysfunctional child. You are much more worthy than that.

You, like everyone and everything that exists on this planet, have a unique purpose, message, and/or addition you are meant to leave behind. Without your message being expressed, there is no way the puzzle of life can be fully complete.

Your AW is not only the holder of, but the expression of, this message, and your life will never be naturally complete, peaceful, or stable until you become one with this purpose. That is why you are reading this book. You realize that there is something greater in you. You may have even experienced it at some point, but you didn't know how to recapture whatever state you were

"The only man who is really free is the one who can turn down an invitation to dinner without giving an excuse."
JULES RENARD

in when you were last one with that purpose.

Sure, you can tire yourself out with activities that are not tied to your true purpose, which so many people do by keeping themselves so busy that they don't have time to feel. You can also desensitize your true feelings through any of a number of prescription drugs or through alcohol, depressants, or stimulants. But none of these substances or activities offers us the true, natural calmness that our lives and our souls seek. That true peace is only available through a oneness with your AW and its unadulterated, universal, free-flowing expression.

The CCM's purpose is completely opposite of the LCM's. For the LCM, because of what we experienced throughout our lives and especially leading up to the so-called 'terrible twos,' equates deep, open, heartfelt expression, which is the mainstay of your AW, as painful. So, your LCM does its best to lead you away from it and instead leads you to one of the many distractions in your life it believes offers you pleasure, which turns out to be a pseudo-relief for your pain.

As mentioned, in this area, like in all others that I'm about to describe, these two parts of you are completely opposite.

THE CCM FEELS

The purpose of your CCM is to first connect the AW with your heart and then, if you so choose, connect it with the hearts of others. The CCM does this through the use of feelings. Thus, where the LCM, because of its conditional nature, needs to think/evaluate or analyze before taking a step, the CCM is not concerned

"Touch and be touched. Feel everything. Open your arms to life. That is why you are here."
PAUL FERRINI
Reflections of the Christ Mind

67

about the result of its actions. It is only concerned with its own expression.

I was flying home from leading a weekend seminar in Florida when the gentleman sitting next to me struck up a conversation. Prior to our discussion, I had been listening to a CD of Jimmy Buffet. When I took off my earphones, the gentleman, who had obviously been able to hear some of what was playing, told me that he had been a longtime, boyhood friend of Buffet's. For the next hour or so, he delighted me with remembrances of Buffet's past. What especially intrigued me were the man's comments about how bad a performer Buffet had been in the initial stages of his career.

"But he didn't care," said the man, "or at least he didn't seem to care about how bad he was because he just kept going back to play over and over, and eventually he became great."

True to the calling of his AW, Buffet obviously was only concerned with the expressions of his feelings. Eventually he got better at expressing them through his lyrics and music. But perfecting his skills for the potential accolades he eventually received was never his primary motivation. Expressing his feelings, true to his AW, was all that mattered.

Artists everywhere, from actors to painters to writers, have all shared similar experiences. Their initial desires to express what they ended up sharing had nothing to do with fame and fortune. They initially did what they did because their AWs just would not leave them alone.

Michelle Branch of Sedona, Arizona, where I live, achieved at the tender age of 18 what most of us never try to experience. By the time she

"Let us be thankful for the fools; but for them the rest of us could not succeed."

MARK TWAIN

was in her teens, she had been singing for several years. But what set her apart from her less successful peers is that she not only expressed the feelings of her AW through singing, but she also listened to its guidance in other areas.

Listening to and adhering to her AW's guidance led her to sneak onto the grounds of Enchantment, an exclusive gated resort community on the outskirts of town, where she heard a well-known record producer was vacationing. Once on the grounds, she stole a golf cart and made her way over to the man's condo. Once there, she slipped a copy of her demo CD under his door, and the rest is history.

So the CCM expressing the feelings of your AW isn't always limited to emotions but oftentimes overflows into actions that provide for a greater sharing of its feelings.

THE CCM IS UNCONDITIONAL

Your CCM is unconditional because it connects with, through your AW, the Ultimate Source – God, your Higher Power, or whatever you may refer to It as being.

It is your AW which serves as the necessary intermediary that transforms the raw, unconditional inspiration of the Ultimate Source into imagery. Imagery is an essential element of human communication because it appeals to one, some, or all of the five senses that the LCM, which controls almost all of our lives, depends upon. Without imagery, your LCM, the gatekeeper, will not allow any messages to pass into or out of your CCM.

"In no other period of history were the learned so mistrusted of the divine possibilities in man as they are now."
GOPI KRISHNA

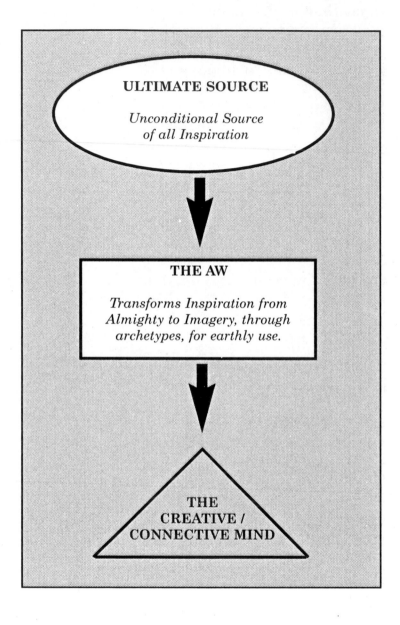

Whether the calling of the Ultimate Source is expressed as a raw inspiration or converted to imagery before being shared, it is and always will be unconditional and, thus, loving and non-judgmental by nature.

YOUR CCM HAS UNLIMITED CAPABILITIES

Have you ever been performing your chosen art form or one of your chosen arts, and inspirations much more intelligent, knowledgeable, or enlightening than you saw yourself as being came streaming out? If so, that was positive proof that you were connected, through your CCM, with your all-knowing, all-seeing AW, which, because of its connection to your Ultimate Source, has unlimited capabilities.

Have you ever been truly inspired or overwhelmed by the work of a specific artist? Then, upon meeting this person or seeing him or her interviewed, being disappointed with their flare or lack of charisma as a personality? Did you then wonder how this person could have produced such a masterpiece yet be so dull or uninspiring?

The truth was that this person did not actually produce whatever it was that had inspired you so. To the contrary, this person had merely released an inspirational expression of the AW. Thus, the artist, because of from where he or she draws, doesn't personally have to be great to produce great art.

It is the norm in our misguided society to believe that individuals 'create' great art. This, of course, puts a tremendous amount of pressure on the artist, especially when deep down inside

"Many of life's failures are people who did not realize how close they were to success when they gave up."
THOMAS EDISON

71

"Style is the man himself."
COMTE de BUFFON

at the base of his or her soul this person realizes that the production comes from somewhere outside of himself or herself. Great pieces of art have always and will always be created at the location where the artist communes with his or her Ultimate Source. This creation is then passed along to the AW, the intermediary between the Ultimate Source and your CCM, where the inspiration is transformed into some form of imagery. But if your CCM is prohibited from freeing the inspiration, it then retreats into the AW where it then stays, relentlessly bugging you until you finally 'release' it.

Yes, 'release' is the proper terminology when referring to the sharing of art. You don't create it because it was actually created by the Ultimate Source and then stored for you in your AW. No, your job is simply to allow your CCM to release it, first to you and then potentially to others.

Then, when it is finally 'released,' it comes with all of the unlimited wisdom, insight, expression, inspiration, color, and depth of the Ultimate Source.

Realizing the difference between 'releasing' and 'creating' in the artistic process takes the pressure off you to create a masterpiece, or to recreate another show-stopper. Isn't it nice to know what our role is? And isn't it nice to know that so much of the responsibility surrounding our art, including all its creation, is out of our hands? In reality, then, all you have to do is allow the Ultimate Source to do all the work while you just release it, sit back, and collect all of the earthly accolades.

Your LCM Is Innately Dominant

Because of its limited earthbound capabilities, your LCM was born to serve the inspirational purposes of the CCM. As alluded to, we were all in perfect alignment with this until the age of approximately twenty-four months. Up until that time, we were one with this connection and one with our feelings as a result. We laughed when we thought something was funny, not to be polite. We cried when we were sad or upset, not to get attention. We smiled when we were happy or joyful, as opposed to doing so out of polite, socially and politically correct routine. When we were upset, we screamed as opposed to swallowing or desensitizing that socially unacceptable emotion with alcohol or some form of extreme physical activity, or legal or illegal medication.

Then, being so open and being so expressive in such a repressive society was no longer acceptable. That is when the LCM, whose job it was to help us integrate ourselves and our purposes — which also translated to keeping us safe and secure — was forced to take over. Life had become a world of mere survival as opposed to a game of expression.

However, despite this emotional slip, the CCM, simply because of the access it has to the Ultimate Source, has been and will always be the dominant portion of you. Your life will never become the living, breathing example of what we can all be until that fact is acknowledged, accepted, and lived. Reversing this unnatural and counterproductive polarity is what this book is all about.

"I have seen you in the sanctuary and beheld your power and your glory."

PSALM 63:2

73

YOUR CCM HOUSES YOUR LONG-TERM MEMORY

Your Long-Term Memory remembers every little detail of your life, from where you were and how you felt during a specific situation, to a tie-in of a fragrance that momentarily passed by you. It is the part of you that when hypnotized and asked to go back to a specific time and place in your life remembers even the most minute detail. It is the portion of you that kicks in when you run into an old friend whom you haven't seen for a considerable period of time, and all of a sudden a flood of memories and recollections of a time long past capture you.

Your LTM is the side of you that your AW draws on to add the color, feeling, personality, and analogy to whatever you share as an artist.

Your LTM is your life recorded in film and in feeling. It is what advocates of the New Age thinking refer to as the Akashic Records, which supposedly have everything you have ever experienced or felt, for however many lives it is that you have lived, recorded and made accessible for retrieval by you and your AW. Your LTM is you, all of your lives, all of your experiences, and all of your feelings. And your LTM is only accessible through your CCM.

YOUR CCM NEVER SLEEPS

I detest being awakened by an alarm clock. I much prefer being awakened by the sun rising and the light it sends through the vaulted ceiling in my bedroom. However, since I am an early

"There is a road from the eye to the heart that does not go through the intellect."
G. K. CHESTERTON

riser who greets the day with meditation, yoga, and usually hiking, if not some other form of physical exercise, waiting for the sun isn't always possible. So, I almost always set my alarm clock to wake me at a certain time. But since I dislike being awakened by the alarm so much, before going to sleep I ask to be awakened slightly before the time my alarm is set to go off.

The system works marvelously, almost always I come out of a REM cycle of sleep two or three minutes before my alarm is set to go off.

What part of me is it that wakes me so I may turn off the alarm before it goes off? The answer is the CCM, because it never sleeps.

Have you ever been awakened in the middle of a deep sleep by a message or scene appearing from a dream that just had to be written down, expressed in some other manner or just felt? If so, what part of you awakened you with the inspiration? The CCM is the one that inspired you to awaken, because it never sleeps.

I think I have made my point about the CCM never sleeping. However, you probably do not realize how important this characteristic happens to be. So important is it, that in my estimation, it is responsible for curing 95% of that which could cause you to disrupt or bring to a complete halt the role of the AW in your life.

"Man came forth from God and must return to God."
BAIRD T. SPALDING
Life and Teaching of the Masters of the Far East

The 95% Solution

It is often considered an accepted fact that to be an artist of any type you either have to be mad beyond belief or disciplined. Of course, those are nothing more than faulty, false excuses tossed out by our well-meaning, but inappropriately educated LCM. All it is attempting to do is distract us from communing with, and thus expressing, the inspirations of our AW.

Sure, an extreme desire by your AW to express itself and to lead you to your real life purpose, when resisted, can turn to madness.

Yes, some people have to be very disciplined to complete tasks. Those are the people, though, who are either performing an activity that they don't enjoy doing, or are involved with one that, for one reason or another, they are frightened to participate in. Because of this book, neither of these dilemmas will continue to be a party to your chosen art forms.

You also have to be disciplined if you have never removed the blockages and/or reversed the polarity of the inappropriate LCM-CCM alignment, which life offered you. But all of that will cease to be a dilemma, as a result of your involvement with this book.

There are, of course, other ways to deal with the inappropriate polarity, which has taken you away from displaying your true artistic potential and purpose. As mentioned before, one of these routes would be through psychotherapy. However, psychotherapy, which can oftentimes take hundreds of consultation hours spread over years of time to accomplish the task, can be expensive time wise and financially.

A major shock, such as a near death experience or the diagnosis of a terminal disease, is another way to get the attention of your LCM, which may turn its attention to the true meaning of your life. However, spiritually, this alternative

"You have to leave the city of your comfort and go into the wilderness of your intuition. What you'll discover will be wonderful. What you'll discover will be yourself."

ALAN ALDA

is normally put into play as a last resort.

Jokingly, as alluded to previously, there is always the frontal lobotomy, which used to be employed liberally as a means of shutting up souls who were screaming way too loudly. In this day and age, that alternative would, of course, be seen as cruel and unusual. We would prefer to just medicate away such inconveniences, no matter how long a person had to stay on whatever drugs or pharmaceuticals were prescribed.

The ultimate state of bliss, peace, and expression that I am referring to was best depicted by Tom Hanks' portrayal of Forrest Gump in the award-winning movie by the same name. A mildly retarded man, Forrest had this amazing ability to move with the flow and calling of his life. Even though he was not a painter, sculptor, writer, actor, singer, or dancer, he was an artist who followed his AW wherever it led him in his life, whether that be to save the life of his sergeant in Vietnam, who became his lifelong friend and business partner; to walk onto the legendary Crimson Tide football team at the University of Alabama, where he became a star; or to start a shrimping business, which he initially knew nothing about but which would eventually make him a multimillionaire.

The most resounding point of this movie had to deal with the convenience of Forrest's mental retardation. Most viewers would insist that the true brilliance of Forrest's life came from the fact that he succeeded despite his affliction. For me, the dramatic point of the movie had to do with the fact that he succeeded not despite his mental retardation, but instead because of it. For it was the deadening of his LCM by the retarda-

"The intellect is always fooled by the heart."
DUC de la ROCHEFOUCAULD

tion that freed him from the usual blockages and LCM dilemmas that many of us struggle with and to which most of us also surrender.

Forrest didn't have that problem, though — did he? No. In his case, the doubts, questioning, and other distractions that usually stand in our way were removed for him by an underdevelopment of his LCM, which is commonly referred to as mental retardation. Am I suggesting that we all swallow a big handful of pills so that we can be like Forrest? No. There is a much simpler and easier way to get in touch with and to live within the flow of your AW. When properly employed, this three-step process, the consistent application of which will be the only disciplined step you need to take, will immediately and proactively cure 95% of the excuses, inappropriate thought patterns, habits, and actions that could keep you from effectively connecting with your AW and, thus, your life's purpose.

When the following method is employed with the options outlined in the section entitled *The Final 5% Solution*, you will have activated the ultimate cure-all for the misaligned, misguided LCM problem that plagues all of our lives.

"When the individual starts for the Promised Land, the land of darkness must be forsaken, forgotten."

BAIRD T. SPALDING
Life and Teaching of the Masters of the Far East

THE THREE "RS" OF WRITING

As I mentioned earlier in this book, I believe I was Divinely led to write. I believe that writing was brought into my life not only to be one of my AW's main forms of expression in my life. But also I was drawn to this one specific outcome so that I could fulfill part of my life's purpose by introducing you to how you can self-induce and awaken your own AW connection. Whether you then choose to put your AW to work through writing or some other form of art is up to you.

The easiest method I know of to put writing to work in releasing your AW, which I have been using for over two decades and which I have been employing with my students nearly as long, I refer to as the *Three Rs.* These Three Rs are: *Reserving Time, Removing All Distractions,* and *Relaxing.*

The consistent application of these Three Rs equate to all the discipline you will need to be able to fulfill the yearnings of your AW.

After you have used this method to transcend the real-to-life barriers of the LCM and connect with your AW, you can then do whatever it is that you want to do with its guidance and inspiration, whether that be playing the piano, singing, dancing, going into politics, business, law, or medicine. But you have to get beyond the constraints of the LCM to do so. When this method is consistently employed, which will take you 3-4 minutes to reach an AW connection each time, all of the potential disaster or procrastination points are removed by completely cleansing you of any and all inappropriate LCM intervention.

For this method to be effective though, it is essential that the Three Rs be utilized each time before you choose to connect with your chosen art form, and each time you review whatever has been released after an expression of an art form. And it is also essential that you remain in your AW connected state during the entire time you are performing your art.

"God tells me how He wants this music played – and you get in His way."
ARTURO TOSCANINI

79

ONCE THE THREE RS OF WRITING ARE EMPLOYED:

➢ *Your connection will be made and the result of which will come bursting through your own unique voice.*

➢ *Any strain of artist's block that you may be suffering from, or that you have ever been plagued with, will be cured immediately.*

➢ *You'll be able to sit down, connect, and be the artist you are at your best anytime and anywhere that you choose.*

➢ *As a result, you will no longer waste hours, weeks, months, and years waiting for the Muse or that "magic moment" to arrive. You will self-induce your God-given insights and be creative NOW!*

➢ *As a result of all of the above, you will become aware that there is a unique, interesting, thought-provoking, potentially awe-inspiring message coming through you, which you can access, enjoy, release, and share at will.*

➢ *Because of the effectiveness of the Three Rs, sharing and expressing your AW will become fun, stimulating, exciting, and life-changing.*

'R' Number One: Reserve time

Have you ever tried to listen to two persons attempting to talk to you at the same exact time? How successful were you in hearing what both had to say? Not very, I'm sure.

You have one set of ears that can only focus on one voice at a time. If you attempt to focus on something other than your AW's voice, you won't be able to hear your Artist Within. To be able to comfortably and effectively hear what your AW has to share, it is essential to reserve a time when your sole intent will be to listen to what it has to say.

How much time is necessary? As much uninterrupted time as possible is best. However, if your schedule is a bit cramped, start with an hour a day, six days a week, at the beginning. Then gradually increase the amount of time by an extra five minutes a day until you wind up connecting a minimum of two hours a day, six days a week.

The time of day at which you choose to connect is also important. The most productive time to write is in the middle of the night. The connection through our CCMs and to our AW appears to be a lot less busy during that time. That's when the LCM is asleep. Writing in the middle of the night is not always the most convenient time, though.

The most convenient time to schedule your sessions is immediately after you rise. During this time, your LCM is still half-asleep.

There are other benefits as well to communing first thing in the morning. Your energy level is higher, which is a plus because you will

"Laziness is nothing more than the habit of resting before you get tired."
JULES RENARD

81

be able to much more easily resist the concerns of your critical side. And, by making connection with your AW as your first activity of the day, you will have a lot less stress because you will be removing, even before the day begins, the all-consuming stress that comes with not living your purpose.

Remember, you are trying to reverse how you relate to the world. In essence, you are trying to replace an ineffective LCM habit with one from the CCM. So consistency is paramount. What this translates to is scheduling your connecting sessions in advance. When you do this, as with the alarm clock analogy I introduced earlier, your AW, which has been calling to be released, will definitely show up.

It does not matter if you commune the same time each day, for the AW is flexible. But scheduling a day in advance is a must. With a pre-established time to express each day, your once desperate AW will quit interrupting you at inconvenient times and awakening you in the middle of the night. Thank God.

Scheduling your AW connection later in the day reduces your degree of effectiveness drastically. The reasons for that are:

> *Your LCM will have become fully awake and active by then.*

> *With social obligations, business and family responsibilities, those times are much more difficult to consistently arrange.*

> *You will have expended your best energy of the day.*

"Do or do not. There is no try."
YODA

82

'R' NUMBER TWO: REMOVE ALL OUTSIDE DISTRACTIONS

Your well-meaning LCM has relied on the availability of outside distractions to keep you from connecting with your AW. It has utilized these tools to capture and also drag away your attention while connected. These distractions have ranged widely from a knock at the door, to a phone call, to the creation of a task that needs addressing immediately.

Because of its underuse, your CCM is not anywhere as strong as your LCM. This will change drastically, of course, by the conclusion of this book. But it is good practice, especially at this stage of your development, to remove all potential distractions from the space in which you plan to connect so your LCM will not use them against your AW.

This means if you have pets, give them the feeding, love, affection, and exercise they so crave before you get started.

If you live with someone, there is probably a very positive reason that you do so. This person and/or people have probably been major, loving assets in your life, who only have your best interests in mind. However, the person or persons will be entering into uncharted waters with you as you venture forth with your AW, and this individual or these individuals may need your assistance in understanding how you may be helped. So, share what you know.

Do so by first expressing how important this phase that you are entering into is to you. Do your best in this regard. Express the passion you have for connecting with your AW. If those who

"Pain is inevitable. Suffering is optional."
M. KATHLEEN CASEY

83

"People hate me because I am a multifaceted, talented, wealthy, intentionally famous genius."
JERRY LEWIS

share your space don't understand or feel as you do, don't become frustrated or alarmed. Not everyone is at the same place at the same time. Their time to connect with their AWs may be just around the bend or way down the road. Either way, your job is to express to the fullest level of your ability how it is that you feel. Whether they catch on or not is out of your hands.

Second, discuss with them your general plans to connect regularly with your AW, and share what it is that you hope to accomplish. Even if you expect that you will be belittled, do it anyway. It's important for you to face what it is that you may be frightened of experiencing, and these persons may just embody exactly that. Not to face a potentially unaccepting response is accepting that a damaging reaction is what you will receive. It's like waving a white flag even before you've entered into battle. It's preordaining a negative outcome. Give whomever it is that you live with the benefit of the doubt. Share openly what it is that you will be doing and why. Since each person has a latent AW stirring inside, you may be surprised at the response. But if you are met with a less than enthusiastic response, so be it. Whatever doesn't kill you does make you stronger and, with the right attitude, you are more than sure to benefit from whatever reaction that is received.

Third, speak openly about your specific plan to connect with your AW on a daily basis.

Fourth, tell those involved what they can do to be of assistance – meaning tell them that what you need during your connection time is a space with absolutely no interruptions. Be adamant and direct. If you do so, they will get the picture.

If you do not, they will be sure to miss your point for the simple fact that they just may not be able to relate to what you are doing and why. If that is the case, do not take it personally. Again, we are all at different places at different times. If we were all at the same place at the same time, there would be no need for different people, abilities, or purposes.

After you have spoken to your roomie(s), make a note to yourself each day before entering into your commune to turn off the ringer on your telephone, the second biggest distraction available to you, and reduce the volume on your answering machine, if you use one.

'R' Number Three: Relax

The final key to being able to make the ultimate of connections is relaxing.

The more and more frustrated or angry or scared we become, the farther and farther we are moved away from the relaxation we need to dull the concern of our LCMs and to hear our AWs.

A state of relaxation has been there every time you have accidentally or innocently made this connection in the past. When you were taking that long drive in the car, and all of a sudden your mind was flooded with ideas, what happened to cause it? With nothing else to do and no one else to worry about, you slipped into your long-distance driving mode and you . . . relaxed! When you relaxed, your LCM did what? Went to sleep, allowing your squashed AW to finally come bursting forth into your CCM.

"Mine eyes have seen the glory of the coming of the Lord; He is trampling out the vintage where the grapes of wrath are stored."
JULIA WARD HOWE

85

The same system was emulated when and if you have awakened in the middle of the night with a desperate need to express. Sleep is an extreme form of relaxation, which lulls your LCM off to sleep, allowing your AW to finally break through and offer you that ultimate of all connections.

The vacation at the beach, in the mountains, or that long plane flight home when all kinds of ideas flooded your consciousness? The same exact thing was happening.

So how do you relax? That is completely and totally up to you. You can meditate, take a cat-nap, do some yoga, go for a walk. The best technique that I know of for achieving the necessary state of relaxation is through the use of the step-by-step routine you have already been exposed to in this book. If you consistently utilize this routine, you will always be able to fully and totally connect through your CCM to your AW.

Whatever method you choose, though, make sure to set aside time to relax, otherwise your LCM will always be in the way.

THE FINAL 5% OF THE SOLUTION

How do we get to the other 5% of the total solution that I promised you? Being unconditional in nature, your AW and CCM seek the wide, open spaces. By nature they are freedom seekers. That is why the lineless pieces of paper you have been using have worked so well up to this point. They supply the unconditional space and free-

"God does not exist apart from you. God is the essence of your being. God dwells within your heart and within the hearts of all beings."

PAUL FERRINI
Reflections of the Christ Mind

86

dom, which are so much a part of your AW and CCM.

Over the last two decades, I have seen the lineless pieces of paper work miracles. On more than several occasions, I have had aspiring authors enter my classes or seminars suffering from what they thought to be incurable writer's block. For months, sometimes years, these people had not been able to write anything of worth. By the time they finally got around to taking one of my courses, they were unnerved or distraught. In each case, I offered them hope through a writing exercise featuring the large, lineless pieces of paper.

As a result of the blankness of this piece of paper I provided, there was no one in class who wasn't feeling uneasy or nervous, especially those suffering from the dreaded 'creative constipation.' Unbeknownst to them, though, it was their LCMs that were creating their reaction. The lack of lines, tangible barriers, rules and regulations, and margins was scaring their conditional sides to death.

Remember the last time your physician prescribed an antibiotic for you?

Well, if you can, you'll also recall that he or she firmly stated that you take 100% of the pills prescribed, because any less than the total prescription would not cure you of your infection.

The infection we are speaking about here, of course, involves the infection that stems from the improper conditioning from your past. Ninety-five percent of the prescription you have requested has already been covered in the form of the Three Rs. Consistent use of these three highly effective techniques completely wipes

"To see a world in a grain of sand and heaven in a wild flower, to hold infinity in the palm of your hand and eternity in an hour."
WILLIAM BLAKE

clean any and all inappropriate LCM intervention, until the LCM can be completely converted into the asset it was meant to be.

This final 5% of the solution is also simple, easy, and inexpensive to employ, and it is effective, so much so that my students have often been left spellbound after using it.

The final 5% solution which I am going to address also revolves around a tool that you have already been employing. It revolves around your use of the lineless pieces of paper.

Why are they so important? Because they offer a space providing unlimited space and freedom, void of LCM rules, regulations, and restrictions. Why is that important? It's important because the Ultimate Source, which comes through your AW and then through your CCM, is unconditional in nature. It doesn't believe in judgment, rules, regulations, or restrictions.

So, what happens when you put a piece of 8 1/2 x 11 lined and margined paper in front of it? At best, it feels limited, pushed, crammed, and shoved into a space that is way too limited for it, and not in any way conducive to its wide-open, free-flowing ways. The worst case scenario leads directly to artist's block, a total shut down of the flow and connection which is your AW. Even with the best case scenario in play, the depth and heart of expression that is the AW, and which makes it so attractive to first you and then to whomever it is that you choose to share your chosen artwork, is non-existent. Remember, it is passion that the public buys. It is the same thing that you buy as well, and if it isn't there for you when you are expressing, you will reject whatever expression it is that is coming through. When

"There is the risk you cannot afford to take [and] there is the risk you cannot afford to take."
PETER DRUCKER

you reject the experience, you are then again rejecting the AW. When the AW is rejected, the entire, silly rejection of your real self and all that is tied to it takes place as well. Then you are caught right back where it was that you began – nowhere.

There are many ways to commune with the Artist Within, and I am sure that you had employed a significant number of alternatives before you began reading this book. However, if what you had put into play before you read this book had been so effective, you would not be reading this now.

The simple truth is that you were missing something or many things. As a result, you were not soulfully satisfied. Frustration may have set in. You went in search of other alternatives. Then, when you did, you stumbled upon this book or, even more amazing, it found you.

You found each other because you were seeking answers, and the book had them. So you've come together for a very significant and timely reason, and now is the time to put those solutions into play. Were it not, you wouldn't be holding this book in your hands and reading this page right now.

I agree that many of the methods I suggest in this book could be seen as unorthodox. But that's a good thing because if the orthodox methods for releasing the AW were so effective, you wouldn't be reading this book.

So when asked by a student initially doubting the process whether using the lineless pieces of paper was an absolute must, I always reply with a resounding, "Yes!" Of course, I know who it is or what part of the student is asking the

"It is only the farmer who faithfully plants seeds in the Spring, that reaps a harvest in the Autumn."

B. C. FORBES

question. That, without a doubt, would be the person's LCM – which cannot stand open spaces and lineless, marginless freedom.

Each of these students complained about the use of lineless pieces of paper only to rave about them after a few writing sessions. Their initial complaints fall in a few different directions, all of which can be overcome with a bit of logic.

First, the people who may complain are initially concerned that the pieces of paper are tough to position for writing or, because I suggest they be as large as possible, they may have a terrible time storing them. This initial complaint can easily be cured by simply folding the paper in half or in fourths.

As far as storage is concerned, even if you were writing an entire book on the largest of the surfaces I suggest, poster boards, and you used 130 of them to do so, they would still fit conveniently behind or under a couch or in a large closet.

Second, the person may complain that he or she strongly prefers creating on a computer. Big problem there though. For no matter how big your screen may be, it is still not as unconditional and as limitless a space as is necessary. As a result, your AW will not have enough room to be fully present.

The expression of art is an all or nothing activity. Either you're all there or not there at all. So being open to your AW halfway on a computer screen still counts as no way.

Third, are the comments that he or she cannot read his or her handwriting. There is a reason for this, of course. Since handwriting is reflective of one's personality and mood, if one is

"God's gifts put man's best gifts to shame."
ELIZABETH BARRETT
BROWNING

90

having a bad day, a bad life, or if one is voicing resentfulness through writing, it will be depicted in a person's handwriting, often causing it to be illegible.

Of course, once you connect with your AW, all of that will change. Initially, your writing will become larger and much loopier. It will begin to dance off in different directions across your paper, as if your AW has just been released from prison, which is exactly what has happened.

Soon after it has had the opportunity to wantonly express itself, your AW will begin to calm down. As it does, your handwriting will shrink in size, but never as small as it may have been initially. Before long you will see a whole different handwriting from what had been there before, symbolizing the new you.

"Far better it is to dare mighty things, to win glorious triumphs even though checkered by failure, than to rank with those poor spirits who neither enjoy nor suffer much because they live in the gray twilight that knows neither victory or defeat."
THEODORE ROOSEVELT

I feel excited about waking up in the morning, and I awake earlier to accomplish my goals. I can only imagine what I can accomplish if I follow through on my commitment to myself and keep it up."

VICKI
Student, New Mexico

BEFORE

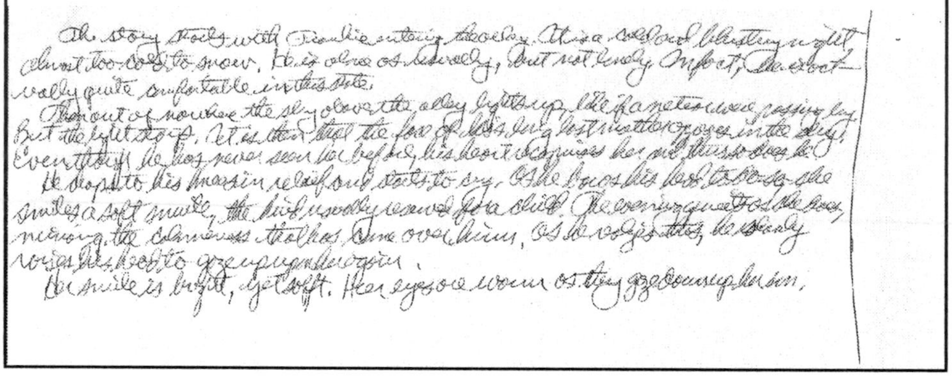

Two handwriting examples showing the transition after reaching the connected state with your AW.

AFTER

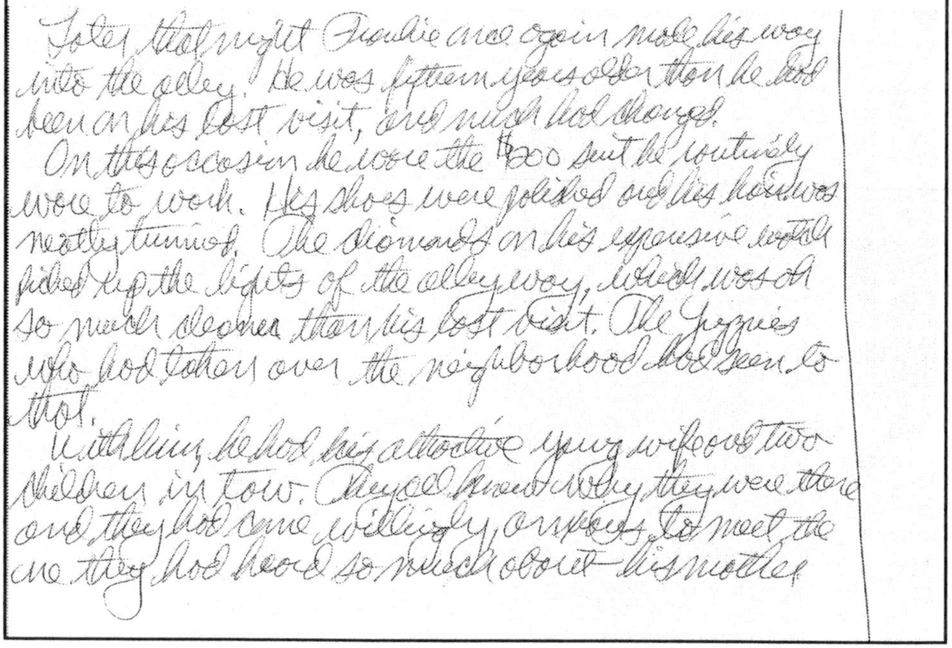

The progression through these stages is natural and representative of the series of releases and recoveries to your new state of normalcy. So, when all of this is transpiring, just sit back, relax, and embrace the fact that all that is happening is natural and good.

Besides offering a conducive surface for your AW to express itself naturally, the large lineless pieces of paper also afford your AW the enhanced perspective it seeks to keep track of its efforts, by knowing where it has been, where it is going, and how all of this applies to the present moment. Since it is important to your AW that this happen all in one glance, many of these large pieces of paper all laid out on one surface accomplishes this task. Computer screens and other sources do not.

The AW's need for this spatial inventory and reflection can best be illustrated by the painter who steps back from his canvas or the sculptor who steps back from her sculpting to acquire an enhanced perspective of where he or she is and where they should go next as a result.

Using these large lineless pieces of paper also offers the tactile connection to their work that every artist needs. They must feel it, breathe it, smell it, and taste it, just like a painter who finds herself covered with paint during a session. This, too, is absolutely necessary for the AW to breath the essence of its efforts and then be able to assimilate where it is going next. Without this unique connection, the AW will not know how to direct itself. As a result, your AW may resort to repeating itself over and over and over again.

Because of the multi-faceted needs that

"Some people don't like it when another says that they've been inspired by God."
NEALE DONALD WALSCH
Communion With God

these lineless pieces of paper offer, many an artist has employed them naturally, including William Faulkner, Walt Disney, you as a child, and your children — when you both drew on the walls. It may have been a much different time, and you may have been in a much different space since you last employed this technique, but your AW is still very much alive and still covets the wide-open, nonconfining, and nonjudgmental spaces provided by these large, lineless pieces of paper.

So productive is this technique that one of my students who came through my class many moons ago even made a very prosperous living by touring the country and helping executive think tanks unlock their enlightened potential through the use of these large pieces of paper, which he referred to as storyboards.

In regard to options for these large, lineless pieces of paper, which we will be using through-out the remainder of this book, I suggest acquir-ing either some 14 x 17 drawing pads or surfaces referred to as poster boards, which can be found in inexpensive ten packs at office supply stores.

I do not endorse drawing pads in a size smaller than 14 x 17 because they are not large enough to offer your AW the full expanse of space that it craves. Nor do I suggest the use of flip charts, especially if you are writing a book. For the sheets found in flip charts are just too flimsy and may not make it through the revision stage that is planned for later.

YOUR ASSIGNMENT

It's now time for you to go out and purchase your chosen writing surface. On your shopping list, also make sure you include the purchase of whatever pen you choose to use, and possibly a backup pen as well.

In regard to the quantity of writing surfaces to purchase, make sure that you have at least 50 sheets on hand of whatever it is that you choose as your chosen surface.

Do not move on until you have completed this essential task.

THE SEMIROUND ROOM AND THE ELEVATOR RIDE TO THE TOP

Step 1. Take the time to follow the preparatory steps at the beginning of this book. Then allow yourself to see that image of yourself standing in front of an elevator door, waiting for it to open. You're alone. The area in which you stand is empty except for you; your favorite music is playing in the background.

Step 2. Visualize the door opening to an empty elevator, with the exception of a tall director's chair that awaits you with your name stenciled on the back of it. You step inside the elevator and ease into the chair. As you do, the door closes behind you, and the elevator rises slowly and comfortably to the very top

"Were you to see only that spark of light within yourself and others, all perception of darkness in your experience would dissolve."

PAUL FERRINI
Reflections of the Christ Mind

95

of its building, where the door opens once again, this time to reveal someone that you feel very close to.

Visualize this person stepping inside the elevator, giving you a big, loving bear hug, lifting you out of the chair, gently taking you by the arm, and escorting you out of the elevator and down a long hallway toward a set of double doors.

Once through the doors, you step into a large amphitheater-type room, with every seat filled. When those in the seats see you enter the room, they all rise to their feet and begin to clap and cheer.

You stop for a moment, as all of this jubilation is taking place, to look around the room. Some of the people you recognize as those who believed in you and who helped you along the way. They are the minority, though, for the rest are made up of all kinds of people whom you do not recognize: young, old, wealthy, poor, attractive, and not so. Some are Americans, some are not. Some are Anglo, some African-American, some Native American. All different types of people are present.

The person who met you at the elevator then leads you onto a rise in the center of the room before the applauding audi-

"The price of greatness is responsibility."
SIR WINSTON CHURCHILL

ence. Once you're there, the cheering of the crowd rises as this special friend or family member bends down to pick up something for you, which most represents whatever it is that you feel called to do, and hands it to you. You take a moment to enjoy the weight of it in your hands. Gaze at it.

"It is inspiration only when it comes direct from God and you let God express through you."
BAIRD T. SPALDING
Life and Teaching of the Masters of the Far East

Step 3. Open your eyes, pick up your pen, and allow how you feel to pour out of you. Remember to blow out any and all tension you may feel and to relax as many times as necessary until the message of this image has thoroughly and completely expressed itself.

―――――――― ⚹ ――――――――

CHAPTER SIX: HOW YOUR AW SPEAKS TO YOU

6

Outside of recognizing that indeed your AW does actually exist and that it is possible to connect with it at will, the next, most significant revelation I am about to introduce deals with how your Artist Within actually communicates with you.

At one time or another, all of us have innocently connected with our AWs, even as adults. However, not understanding the method in which it speaks to us may have caused us to reject the message or the connection by thinking ourselves to be crazy or, even worse, possessed.

Please rest assured though that what I am about to describe, as unusual as it may be to a logical way of thinking, is actually quite normal in dealing with the AW.

What I am about to describe stems from the

"Deeply embedded in your psyche is the call to awaken."
PAUL FERRINI
Reflections of the Christ Mind

term *archetypes,* first made popular in the modern world by psychotherapist Carl Jung. Jung used the term archetypes to describe images shared with us by our subconscious. Because of their vivid richness and color, these images could be interpreted from many different angles and, as a result, oftentimes possessed a myriad of meanings.

To begin with, for our use, it's best to define the type of archetypes we will be working with as *symbolic representations of deep-seated, multifaceted, universal meanings and/or communications.*

As mentioned, it is essential to understand these forms of communication, just as it is necessary to understand the basis of whatever language it is in which someone is speaking to you. This is no different than if one chose to attend a lecture by a speaker who only spoke French. To understand what this person would be saying, it would, of course, be essential to understand French. To reject the French language, in this case, would also be to reject both the speaker, and not only how he or she chose to convey his or her work, but the message as well.

The same holds true with the communications of the AW. It has a distinct way in which it communicates with you. To understand how it communicates is not only to accept the message but the messenger. To do the opposite, of course, is to reject both the AW and what it has to say.

The ultimate goal of all communication from your AW is always spiritual evolution for you and all whom it touches. This is so because our primary purpose as human beings is to narrow and, we hope, eventually remove for good all that stands between us and God. Thus all communication with our AWs is meant to move us along more swiftly toward that goal. Understanding this will enable us to better understand the images, influences, and situations that are taking place in our lives so we will be less likely to reject them and instead see them as the Divine-led lessons that they happen to be.

The AW does this through two distinctly different types of archetypal persons, situations, or circumstances. Again, it is important for you to acknowledge and understand this so you do not reject where the AW is taking you and why it is taking you there. For it is through these persons, situations, or circumstances that it brings to your life what it is trying to communicate, something of dire and timely significance to you.

The first brand of archetype is the *Transformational Archetype* or TA. Even though both archetypes are good at calling and encouraging you to evolve, this specific type is designed to help you grow through the removal of bias. The bias this type of archetype attempts to remove is a bias against yourself, which keeps you from loving yourself as deeply as possible. It is essential that this self-love be in place and match the intensity of the Ultimate Source. For if it is not, then you will reject the flow of unconditional love, abundance, creativity, and expression destined for you from the Ultimate Source.

The familiarity or trust that you feel as the result of this type of connection allows the message being conveyed by your TA to strike a very deep, personal note.

Examples of when your AW was attempting to contact you on an issue of a very deep person-

"America's best buy is a telephone call to the right man."
ILKA CHASE

103

"The door is never closed to you or anyone else."
PAUL FERRINI
Reflections of the Christ Mind

al nature vary widely. When you have had a dream in which someone you know, love, and trust was present is a good example. A dream played out against a familiar backdrop such as the neighborhood in which you grew up or a school you attended is another. A character whom you recognize that pops into your mind if you are writing a book or short story is still another example.

The array of connections you have already experienced in this regard are endless. One of the most important things to keep in mind, though, is that your TAs usually appear in the form of someone or something with which you are familiar or trust, so as to be able to reach way deep down inside you and to deliver a message. That message is always one of love: love for yourself.

Here are some examples of how this connection has touched the lives of others.

CASS

I decided, after taking one of Tom's seminars as part of a local college's continuing education offerings, to buy his book and go through the exercises myself. One thing that still amazes me about this process is that I completed all the exercises! I doubt that I have ever completely followed through on any book's program, but I did with this one. I followed through all the way to a retreat in Sedona and sending out query letters.

The exercises to meet my TA led me to people I had always respected: Dorothy Dunnett, Albert Einstein, John Lennon. Then, during a meditation, I noticed, out of the corner of my eye, a jester, a joker. Dressed as a harlequin, he poked around at my brain and my thinking, letting me know that I let too much go by; that I paid very little attention to the more important thoughts that rambled across my internal screen. Because jesters are historically able to tell a monarch the Truth without repercussion, and because my maiden name is Little, I watched out for his messages. I think he prodded me to the next stage.

I met my AW doing the exercises in the book. The best way I can describe the situation is to compare it to Anne Rice sitting in a room interviewing Louis. Midway through my own experience, I was convinced that the same thing had actually happened to get *Interview with the Vampire*. I was walking through my living room, and she popped up as a voice in my head that told me very clearly what I was thinking! I just grabbed some index cards and started listening and transcribing. The important part was that I listened to her. I think she's been there for a while, but I had stuffed her down under daily concerns.

She, Cara, was also the first *Primary Archetype* (PA). In many ways, she was me, but clearly stating what I/she wanted to accomplish. She had my wishes and hopes, but she could actualize them; she could have all the good luck. She had problems, but she could work on them. She introduced me to Billy Joe. He introduced both of us to Barb, who introduced all of us to Psue.

The four characters let me play with them while they played with each other. Although the

"I keep the telephone of my mind open to peace, harmony, health, love, and abundance. Then, whenever doubt, anxiety, or fear try to call me, they keep getting a busy signal – and soon they'll forget my number."
EDITH ARMSTRONG

105

information I was developing through them was complex, I enjoyed keeping all the threads juggling on the stage of life with them. I especially appreciated the time I set aside daily to play and work with them. They always came out, and they always had something to say. The book developed rapidly. I hate outlines, but one day I had 46 chapters outlined in about 20 minutes! As I continued, I made very few changes to the outline.

Part of what has happened since I took this ride has been that I started doubting myself again. I have a ton of Connection Breakers constantly prowling my perimeters since I was in NYC on 9/11/01; I was able to push them back for nearly nine months with my new friends, but daily life scares me. Even though I know my PAs can get me out of the cage, I'm afraid. The four characters are not too fond of doubt, so they are hibernating. But I know that's all they're doing — they're not gone.

However, I have actualized many of Cara's wishes! Many of the things we wrote about in the book have happened to me. She is a teacher, and so am I. I got a job teaching, and I haven't gone back to the book. I've realized that maybe the book was not about being published, but about getting my own dreams on the page so I could go after them. I do, however, feel like I have The Gift, as in Saul Bellow's book, because I also have a manuscript that I can get publishable with some more work. How many people have got 46 good chapters lying around?

Thank you, Tom...and Cara, and Billy Joe, and Barb, and PSue.

"The successful people are the ones who can think up things for the rest of the world to keep busy at."

DON MARQUIS

JOHN

Early in the summer of 2001, I spent one week asking God to introduce me to my Transformational Archetype. Every night before going to bed and every morning for six days I would read a page-long written request. Each day, nothing. Finally Friday night arrives, and just before climbing into bed, I add the following to the statement I had been reading to God for five days now; "Okay, God, I keep asking and not receiving. What's the deal here? I've done everything in my realm utilizing the big three. 'Ask and you shall receive, knock, and the doors will be opened to you, seek and you shall find,' but still you have not answered." I then went to sleep with the expectation that this was my night to finally receive. Didn't happen. I woke up the next morning and realized that still nothing had come my way. Got up, went into the bathroom, and did something I don't usually do once I'm awake. I went back to bed.

I laid there snuggled up under the warm blankets, just thinking about not receiving. I was a bit upset with what had not transpired. A few moments of silence and not thinking, all of a sudden a name comes before me in the form of a whisper, 'Tal'man.' What a weird name I thought. It came back again, this time a bit louder. 'Tal'man.'

What's that, I thought. Oops, that's his name, Tal'man. He is the guide I'd been asking to be introduced to for a week now. "Okay Tal'man, it's been a long time I've been waiting for you, so now let me ask you some questions." I laid there on my bed asking questions about

"The artist is nothing without the gift, but the gift is nothing without the work."
EMILE ZOLA

107

"Only the curious will learn and only the resolute overcome the obstacles of learning. The quest quotient has always excited me more than the intelligence quotient."
EUGENE S. WILSON

meditation, receiving one answer after another.

That was the last time I encountered Tal'man until the weekend following September 11, 2001. A day in time most of us will never forget. The workshop was titled, *The Author Within* hosted by Tom Bird and expected cohost, Dan Millman. Due to the 9/11 situation, Dan, however, was not able to attend so we got the full Monty with Tom Bird.

Tom taught us the concept of finding our Transformation Archetype. On day three, we started the morning off with a few brief words and then we were turned over to our TA. For the next three hours I had an exchange with Tal'man that revealed a great deal about physical life. Questions were answered dealing with utilizing the senses for meditation and also for writing. The questions were all prephysical-based and the knowledge that I received about the Universe was unreal. I wrote well over two to three thousand words. I was on a roll, and my hand was really tired at the end.

This experience inspired me to no end and has changed my life forever. It broadened my belief and understanding that we do have guides, angels, masters, etc., waiting there for our beck and call. My TA is there for my undivided attention anytime I'm ready to finish completing my lifetime work. He's there every step of the way with my writing. What I have learned is that I have to ask all the questions. But I can tap into him whenever I need to. That includes driving down the road.

Let me share an interesting story with you as an example of this. One morning when climbing into the shower I had a strange thought.

"Don't drive in the fast lane today." Weird, I thought. What's that all about? I ignored it. While driving to work, as I do every day, I drove in the fast lane. Halfway to work, I hit a divot in the road and blew out my front left tire. After pulling over to the right side of the highway, I realized I needed to walk a mile up the road to find a phone. While walking along the highway, I decided to invoke my TA. I kept saying, "Okay, Tal'man or God, whichever wants to answer, what's the message behind this flat tire?"

I got all the way to the gas station at the next off ramp and made a call to Triple A. They asked me to meet the driver at the car so I began walking back. "Hey, guys, what's up? You haven't answered my question. I'm invoking the big three and you're not answering."

Moments later, I happened to look down and spot a nickle and a penny. I picked them up and held them in the palm of my hand. "Okay," I said, "what's the message you're trying to give me in the six cents? Oops," I said with a laugh. "I get it. *Use your Sixth Sense.*"

MARY

I am one of the 81% Tom describes who feel they have a book inside of them, but the true desire to write did not occur until I was inspired by divine guidance. My background is mostly math and science, and I have worked in research and sales. Whenever I have read a good book and been absorbed in the story, I have always thought it would be fun to write, but never thought that I would. When I received the guidance to write, I thought, well, I had written

"Surrender is inner acceptance of what is without reservations."

ECKHART TOLLE;
The Power of Now

109

*"The predominance of mind is
no more than a stage in the evolution of consciousness. We need
to go on to the next stage now,
as a matter of urgency; otherwise, we will be destroyed by
the mind, which has grown into
a monster."*

ECKHART TOLLE
The Power of Now

many term papers in school and reports since,
but a book? When I started to write, it was amazing. The information I was receiving came pouring out of me, and I was not only consumed, but
hooked. Who knew there was an author within
me?

In 1998 I decided to simplify my life and
spend more quality time with my soul. This led
to the discovery of a whole new person. I have
always been spiritual, with a deep faith in God.
The knowledge of what I have known to be true
has been with me since I can remember, around
age three. I live in a rural area, and behind my
home is where my connection to the Universe
became even stronger. This would usually occur
around sunrise while I was watering trees. There
is this one little mesquite tree that was fine the
first year it was planted then it began struggling.
Mesquite trees grow naturally and are very
hearty, so it was odd that this little tree was having trouble. I received most of my initial guidance while watering this one tree. The tree
would do well and then would seem to struggle,
and this cycle would continue to happen. I
noticed, looking back over the past several years,
that this little tree's growth has seemed to paral-
lel my advancing spiritual growth.

My TA is Jesus. He has always been a part of
my life, but his presence became very strong the
spring of 1999. The overwhelming feeling of
unconditional love surrounded me (while watering the tree). I found all of this so amazingly
comfortable. My life, thoughts, wants, and needs
started to change over the next year and a half. I
then found myself at a crossroad. I knew I no
longer wanted to continue living the life I was

living. A good life, earning a good living, fulfilled materially, but pointless. Then 9/11 occurred and my work came to a standstill. This was the first time I really stopped and took a break without being concerned about business. I started reading a stack of books that had been waiting to be read.

By the time January came, the thought of returning to work was not appealing. I had become more connected to my inner self and Jesus, and loved the space I was in. By summer, information was pouring through me, and in October I knew I was going to be writing. The guidance was strong, but I was unsure of me. I was not a writer, plus, who was I to be writing a message directed by Jesus? It took me until January to become comfortable with the idea. The guidance to write was so strong that I allowed it to direct me without question. I would be awakened early in the morning, usually around 2:30, bright and alert, with the information pouring from me, and I would write whatever I was receiving.

I wrote about 80% of the rough draft of the text in six weeks. Although the flow was constant, it came in pieces. In mid-March I organized my notes and began to type. Besides not having considered myself a writer, I am not a typist, but that did not seem to matter either. Early in the process I started meditating prior to beginning, and this made a great deal of difference. As I would type, more information would come to me. The text had a life of its own, and I would become so consumed that my life would be the book for days at a time. When I would go back and read what was on paper, I would be

"The question is not what you look at, but what you see."
HENRY DAVID THOREAU

111

amazed. I would know that I wrote it, but remembered few of the details. I became overwhelmed with the information I was receiving, so I stopped to take stock of my thoughts the end of April.

The end of May I went to see Julia Ingram, M.A. for what I described to her to be enhancement for my life. She is well known for her hypnotherapy and regression therapy. The session with her was no less than amazing. Talk about connecting. It took about ten days after seeing her to begin writing again. The effect this had on my writing was amazing. I had been holding back putting on paper some of what I was receiving. I revised and added much to what had been written, doubling the volume, during the next three weeks.

During this explosive time, I attended Tom's seminar. I thought I was going to learn about publishing, but I learned so much more. He talked about what I had been experiencing, and this gave me even more confidence. I only wish that I had read his book before I started. I know that I would have been more organized and more encouraged sooner.

As I continued to write, the information continued to add to what I had written in January and February, and I no longer held back. I stopped writing two more times due to being overwhelmed. I learned so much during this process that I had to take time to absorb it. I thought my life had changed prior to writing the book, but the changes during and since continue to amaze me. Besides the spiritual experience, which has been nothing less than amazing, humbling, and fulfilling, I fell in love with writing.

"If error is corrected whenever it is recognized as such, the path of error is the path of truth."
HANS REICHENBACH

Realizing the creative expression from within has been the most fulfilling and satisfying experience of my life to this point. I know the experience would not have occurred without the inner connection. Tom has found the key to writing, or any creative experience. I would describe my experience as beyond belief, but it is the most comfortable space I have ever been in.

HARRY

Eagle Soars High in Peru

I didn't know for what I was searching or why I was there when I traveled to Machu Picchu, Peru, holy city of the Incas. I only knew that feelings long bottled up inside were bubbling to the surface in rapid succession as I was finally forced to face my writing demons.

It was a talented group of soul searchers accompanying me on this trip that would help me unlock my fears and stifle the critical giant that loomed deep inside the corridors of the mental maze I had been lost in for months.

My first TA came as a flying eagle stopping to feed baby eaglets high among the Andes.

It appeared in a vision after meeting a Native American artist specializing in sacred jewelry. He provided me the medallion, which became a conduit to the metaphysical journey that day.

Holding the medallion close to my heart and closing my eyes, a mental image loomed clearly that midmorning, right in the middle of a conference break. People scattered around the room were unaware of my experience. I was quite startled, fearful, and yet, exhilarated at the

"To the dull mind all of nature is leaden. To the illumined mind the whole world sparkles with light."

EMERSON

113

same time. What was even more surprising was how quickly I drew the meaning of what the eagle's mission was telling me.

The eaglets were the baby boom generation seeking nourishment and answers. I was the eagle feeding them, and the food I was providing was the message and information that I was to write in the days ahead. This message confirmed the urges I had to write and gave me confidence to proceed in attending a writing retreat and hiring a writing coach.

Statue of Liberty – Freedom and Creativity

My second Peruvian TA experience came during a "Healing Touch" session with a registered nurse that traveled from her work at Canyon Ranch in Tucson, AZ. She utilized her skills in reading body vibrations and body heat to help me release sore neck and arm muscles that had been troubling me for three years. Sue also took me on a spiritual journey that included passing through a doorway to meet and explore my feminine side.

My female side came to me as the Statue of Liberty, holding high a lighted torch to show the way. Talking through telepathy, she explained that the path to creativity required the freedom to let go of the past. Freedom to unshackle restricting ideas and values. Freedom to let go. Freedom to just be me.

Her size, stature, and courage displayed that feminine qualities don't have to include weakness, a fear that had kept me from my exploring my female side. This experience told me that my writing creativity comes from the way I look at things emotionally. I now choose to feel the world as well as see it. Achieving a broader mindset

"He who has a why to live can hear almost any how."
NIETZSCHE

114

has become one of my writing goals.

Tough Guy, Papa Hemingway

Shortly after visiting with the Statue during my healing session, I came across famous writer Ernest Hemingway hunched over his typewriter. He typed me messages:

"You could be better (writer) than I was because you believe in God."

"I can help you if you let me."

He also told me he handled depression and the fear of failure through his drinking. His stormy relationships with others, and especially women, sharpened the emotional side of his writing and was how he painfully overcame his feminine side while writing.

Visiting Hemingway's Home in Key West has always been magical. It now has significant meaning when I go there, as it conjures up my past encounters with this legendary hero of the literature community.

Although I am presently dormant in my writing, I view it as merely a transformational stage. Much like the giant aspen groves. These trees provided beauty, daytime shade and night-time warmth throughout much of the year. However, they spend a considerable amount of time in the winter "dead to the world." All of this time, these beautiful trees remain connected to each other through their root systems in one of the world's largest living organisms. One grove in Utah measures over one hundred square miles. I remain connected to the world, although not actively through my writing at the moment.

"Our greatest happiness does not depend on the condition of life in which chance has placed us, but is always the result of a good conscience, good health, occupation, and freedom in all just pursuits."
THOMAS JEFFERSON

"For me a picture should be something likeable, joyous, and pretty...yes, pretty. There are enough ugly things in life for us not to add them."
PIERRE AUGUSTE RENOIR

FRANCES

I met my TA in one of Tom's seminars of The Writers' Success Series on March 10, 2001. (Yes, the spring before the world exploded.) The Native American-looking, with blue eyes and long black hair, dude's name was/is "Magic." (Clumsy sentence, but you get the picture.)

I wrote up that amazing encounter, submitted it to the editor and it was published in the Roundtable, vol. 4, issue 8 – March 19, 2001, should you wish to look it up and read it in its (long) entirety.

I still implicitly trust Magic and His continuing presence in my life. I remember several important things he spoke to:

1) "Let go...of all my pictures, expectations of what my creative writing process is supposed to be, look like and feel like...and trust my own process; trust the transformative, transcendent energy of my Inner Resources: power, healing, love, and wisdom." And, I'd add at this point, the "warrior's spirit" of self-discipline, overcoming obstacles, and perseverance! ("To let go and trust" was/is not easy for an impatient, high-strung, obsessive-compulsive/perfectionist type like me.)

2) By engaging wholeheartedly in the adventure of writing my first novel, I would be "entering into a Sacred Relationship, a space of Belonging. Never forget that and honor it as such – no matter what." (Like a "marriage," based upon contract and commitment; conflict and negotiation; appreciation and gratitude; and true, abiding, but ever-evolving love.)

The fear that kept/keeps coming up was/is by

paying deep attention to the creative writing process, I was making myself visible, transparent to "the world" and, therefore, vulnerable. Yes, many revelations later, there is still much trembling, angst, and many ouches during the dark nights of the ego! (I believe that the soul/spirit as the authentic Self is never in the dark; it's always in the Light. It's the fear-bound ego that gets in the way of that Self – just like in a marriage!)

3) "Embrace the paradoxes and give voice to the creative tension and flow of the images and emotions contained within them. Engage the creative process, its emergent characters, images, and storyline with passion, heart and meaning."

Wow, I sure have been there, done that! And am, of course, still with it! And, oh yes, let it all "breathe" – like everything alive, the writer and his/her characters all go through phases of contraction and expansion; intense intimacy or engagement and requiring space or incubation. Allow for that process in its own natural rhythm. Don't force anything to happen; just allow. (Magic just checked in and wrote that. I kid thee not...) Goes for all other areas of my life too, I say!

4) "Know that my writing is an ongoing conversation among Self, Other, and the World. Inspiration is as vast and deep as the Well of Stars: go there, reach in with an open heart, a courageous heart and drink passionately and deeply of the Divine. Then write..."

Finally, I would add, Magic still reminds me to listen to your sage advice, Tom:

"Sit down, shut up, breathe, and write!"

"We will never do anything 'til we cease to think about the manner of doing it."
WILLIAM HAZLITT

117

And, oh yes, "Don't worry about it," when all the nah-nah-nah's come up. (AKA the Inner Critic. But I've now trained that entity like a rambunctious hound dog: to "Sit, stay..!" outside the door 'til I call him. He grumbles, whines, then lies down and waits, rolling his eyes at me but quiet. When I'm jolly good and ready, it's "Okay! Here, Boy..!" and in Nah-Nah-Nah bounds, barking and slobbering all over sections and chapters I must indeed rework. So, in effect, we have a kind of partnership. When I'm done, I throw him a bone then take him for a run around the lake. My kitty-cats don't like him one bit! They fuzz up and hiss at him. I can't blame them, but my Inner Critic/hound dog has been trainable... (Smile.)

I'm still practicing Magic's teachings; but not yet a "Master" of either the writing process, the book still in progress, nor of my (ego or little) self! I will say this, though, writing this first novel, the IWP, and you, Tom, have transformed me and my life. I simply cannot not write. And the beat goes on. Thank you, Tom...and The Magic Within.

JIMMIE LOU

I first met my TA in Tom's one-day, mid-October SCC writing workshop in Scottsdale, Arizona. After teaching us how to relax and connect with our AW, he had us write fast on a large piece of paper for 15 minutes. I was very surprised as I wrote fast; the feelings just started to flow out of me through my pen. I knew I had wanted to write for a long time. I cried.

I easily recognized connecting with my TA

"Our doubts are traitors, and make us lose the good we oft might win by fearing to attempt."
SHAKESPEARE

again the second time at home, sitting on my back porch, feet up, eyes closed, smiling. My first reaction was "Wow!" And I've had that same reaction many times now. This experience made me feel empowered. I saw how much I had within me that needed to be expressed. I felt the joy of letting my true feelings flow onto paper. I felt happy and would smile or laugh or cry at times. Another unusual feeling was that when an angry thought came up, it was immediately followed by a forgiving attitude – a more empathetic or caring attitude toward that person.

As I practiced connecting with my AW, it became more and more automatic. I now only have to imagine sitting on the patio, feet up, eyes closed, smiling, and I can easily connect again. I still do the Three Rs, but I connect a lot more quickly.

Even when I'm just relaxing, I get connected! Like right now, I have to go to sleep – it's 11 p.m., and I have to teach tomorrow! I used to have a rule for myself to be in bed by 9 or 10 since I'm a teacher and must be rested to deal with kids! But writing and connecting makes me need less sleep, and I'm still more energized than before! I have a new sensitivity to kids, and people in general. I listen more, respond more freely, laugh more, smile more, love people and life more. And for some reason, even tragedies seem to be less tragic because I feel an eternal hope for the future. I'm more optimistic and share my optimism. I notice that those who knew me before now look at me like something is different about me – they give me a smiling, side-glance, like "Something's different about her!" Then I enthusiastically tell them what I'm

"When an emotional injury takes place, the body begins a process as natural as the healing of a physical wound. Let the process happen. Trust that nature will do the healing. Know that the pain will pass and, when it passes, you will be stronger, happier, more sensitive and aware."
        PETER McMILLIAMS
        How to Survive the Loss
        of a Love

119

learning about my CCM, LCR, AW, etc.

Another observation is that I can clearly see the differences between my connected writing and my LCM writing. Both are needed at different times, but the CCM writing is a lot more fun. Even when doing research writing, however, I'm finding that my AW can make it much more interesting than before. It seems my LCM is learning from my CCM!

What is interesting is that I have learned that my book about my mother and grandmother's unique lives is a more exciting story than I first thought! And it's catchy — as I talk to family members about my story, they become excited and enthusiastic also. I've made long distance contact with some relatives I haven't talked with in as many as 40 years! My whole life seems to be becoming more "connected!"

Finally, and maybe most important, I am more at peace now. Before these experiences, I was not able to express myself to those closest to me — my family. But now that I am more open with my true self and how I feel, I am becoming more open with them.

I am looking forward to even more unique writing experiences, connecting with my CCM, and writing more and more freely! I look forward to seeing "What's next?"!

TAS, YOUR UNIQUE PURPOSE AND PAS

The last component to keep in mind about TAs is that since their presence is designed sole-

MAE WEST: *For a long time I was ashamed of the way I lived. Did you reform?*
MAE WEST: *No; I'm not ashamed anymore.*

ly to convey a message of unconditional love to you, they, unless you choose to share somethingof a cathartic nature, are not meant to be shared for public consumption.

These images, circumstances, feelings, and situations appear, strike you deeply, remain until their job has been completed and the shift that they sought has been completed, and then, they leave, making room for the second brand of archetype, the *Primary Archetype* or PA.

Even though at times it is almost impossible to believe that this is true, you have a very unique and special purpose to live, an individualized message to share, which is why your AW, who is the courier of that message, exists in the first place. It is then the message conveyed to you by your AW, whether it be a certain splash of color against a canvas, an image one sees in a block of granite, or an outrageous character who you have never seen before and who stumbles into your life, that embodies your purpose on this Earth, and which is meant to be shared in whatever art form it is that you choose. However many or however few you affect is not of importance. For the Ultimate Source, such as Paul's meeting in the New Testament with the mysterious stranger on the road to Damascus and how that drastically changed his life and the world, has He, She, or Its own plan and way of doing things. Your job is simply to become one with the message and allow it to be released through you.

So, what it all comes down to is that the TA is meant to convey a deep spiritual message to you for personal transformation, while the *Primary Archetypes* (PA) exist to share a deep, moving method with the world through you.

"It takes two to speak the truth – one to speak, and another to listen."
HENRY DAVID THOREAU

As a result, PAs are vastly different from TAs. Here is how.

First, PAs appear in the form of someone or something you either don't know or do not recognize.

Second, as mentioned, their purpose is not to transform you, but instead to share a message that in some large or small way will transform the world.

Third, in this way, they can be viewed as angels or spiritual guides. The combination of these three components can often be both shocking and exhilarating. Indeed, shocked, but wildly excited, is how I would best categorize my students' typical reaction to the initial appearance of a PA .

When I work with a student through my *Intensive Writing Program*, he or she is responsible for checking in with me at an allotted time several days a week. A student whom I am currently retained by, called me one day during her appointed time and told me that she began hearing a woman's voice in her head during her writing time, and that the lady was speaking to her in an English accent. Concerned, but curious, my student wasn't quite sure what to do.

Having been through the experience myself and with my students thousands of times, I knew exactly what was happening. My student had turned the corner on the cathartic end of her writing, outrun the need for her PAs, and she was now ready to go headlong into releasing her life-transforming message. How did I surmise this? Because my student had never heard the voice of the woman calling out ever before.

The student to which I am referring was a

"This is above all: To thine own self be true."
SHAKESPEARE

Ph.D. psychotherapist. Those with advanced degrees oftentimes, because of their training, can be overly critical of the ways of the CCM and of the AW. So, they often need a little nudge to insure they are moving in the correct direction. She was no different. In fact, she was the first of three students that week to experience the same situation. Another was a psychiatrist and the other was a holder of a master's degree, to whom I offered the same advice.

I gave this student of mine a name by which she could refer to her voice, which offered her a certain sense of security. Another PA, a male counterpart, also appeared. I also offered her a few areas in which I suggested she explore the identity of these two individuals, why they had come together, and what it was that they were meant to do.

Responding to the calling of her AW, the student leapt right into the exercise, and the voice of the female PA, having gained the acceptance and opening she craved, came pouring through. Immediately, my student found herself completely immersed in the background and voice of the character. Within no time at all, she knew more about this PA, who was more than happy to answer whatever questions were posed to her, than she did about most of her clients. This PA was now where she needed to be, in full control. After having seized control of the situation, the female PA renamed her male counterpart and told my student all that she could possibly want to know about herself, him, and the story that they were going to write together.

The above description does not constitute an uncommon occurrence. In fact, most of you have

"I am large, I contain multitudes."
WALT WHITMAN

123

"I can believe anything, provided it is incredible."
OSCAR WILDE

probably already experienced this in one way or another with your dreams. The simple reason that this form of communication may not have worked for you as well as you have wanted comes directly as the result of not understanding and, thus, not being able to give in to that which was connecting with you. This lack of understanding about what was actually taking place with these PAs, spirit guides, and/or angels, caused your controlling LCM, in one way or another, to panic, which in turn shut down your connection.

Somewhere along the way, your LCM justified its extreme actions by categorizing you as nuts or at least unstable. Then, from that point forward, you would see any similar experiences as being crazy. This reaction would then steer you away from re-experiencing anything like this ever again.

All our lives can't be as pleasing as best-sellers. However, understanding this form of AW-based/CCM connection is the key. An understanding or misunderstanding in this area directly determines whether one's LCM accepts the experience for what it is or rejects it because of a lack of knowledge. The more one leans toward the latter, the slower, more difficult, challenging, less productive, and potentially painful the experience will be.

To further illustrate this point, allow me to share with you a story about a bestselling author. A few years ago, before making an evening presentation at the University of Missouri in St. Louis, I was hanging out in my hotel room relaxing and doing some channel surfing, when I ran across "The Oprah Winfrey Show." On this occasion, Oprah was featuring the work of an author who had just written a bestseller.

Oprah, as she always does, prepared extensively for the interview of this author, backwards and forwards. She also loved the book, which was why the author was on the show in the first place.

Oprah, in her typical enthusiastic demeanor, asked her guest how he had been able to write a novel for the layperson on a topic that had hit home so effectively, something that so many others had been trying to do for so long, all of whom had failed miserably. I believe that Oprah was probably trying to evoke some sort of technically laden response from the author about how he had discovered or employed a magic formula to go where no author had ever gone before. Instead, the mild-mannered guest surprised even me with the candor and directness of his response.

He simply told the story of how, during one of his routine, daily writing sessions, the image of a woman appeared. He then followed his intuition and took some time to explore the background of the woman who sought to communicate so very openly with him. As he did that, he gained a greater knowledge of her until he soon arrived at the point where he trusted her. Once that took place, he literally handed the pen over to the woman and allowed her to write his bestseller through him.

His decision, of course, paid off for him, as the book eventually landed on every major national bestseller list in the country. As a result, his fledgling writing career was transformed to one of a bestselling author. Now, every

"I came to the conclusion that one of the reasons why I'm so blessed, I think, is because I reach so many people, and you never know whose life you are touching or affecting. And so, because your blessing come back to you based upon how you give them out...that's why I'm so.... You know what I'm saying? You get it? Okay, good."
OPRAH WINFREY

book the author pens, even before it's released, is a bestseller. All of this came about because he chose to listen to and to give in to the experience, which allowed the book to be written for him and through him, and vaulted him to national prominence, which he had obviously been unable to do on his own.

The guest was a writer who wanted to be a bestselling author. He tuned to the same exact connection that I have been speaking about and his prayers were answered. This will also work for you, whether becoming an author or something else is what you want to do. Understanding how your AW attempts to communicate with you through your CCM is essential, though, so that you give in to the experience and, thus, allow it to do its work for you.

As you may or may not have already experienced on your own, once you give over to a PA, he, she, or it will literally do whatever it is that needs to be done for you. When this happens, you will experience a few unique reactions.

First, when whatever art that you are involved with initially begins to come through you, it will have been waiting anxiously for years, if not decades.

Second, it will also have been used to being an opportunist, ready to take full advantage of whatever situation it can seize, no matter what time or day you give it to be released.

What this means is that when you first tie into it, it will come flying out at warp speed. It is important during these initial times to keep in deliberate control of your breathing. *If you can control your breathing, you can control an inappropriate reaction to any situation.* So, no matter how you feel, keep breathing deeply. Keep breathing smoothly, through your nose. Make sure to blow out any tension that you may be feeling by taking in as deep a breath as you can and then exhaling it quickly. It also helps to envision whatever tension it is that you are feeling leaving you at this time in the reflection of a color, shape, or both.

Setting a specific time to commune with your AW each day, as we have already discussed, will help immediately. Once your AW realizes that your CCM will be providing it with the desired and needed opportunity to release its message each day, it will no longer panic, push you beyond your human limits with an inhuman speed of release, and it will become the compassionate and caring friend that it truly is. It will show up specifically at the time you have designated to begin your session. Then, though reluctantly at first, it will draw each of your writing sessions to a close either at the end of your allotted time frame or immediately after whatever quota of expression you may have set for yourself. This leaves you with a real emotional and spiritual high.

There also will be no more untimely interruptions by the AW when it senses an opportunity to speak and takes advantage of it by coming through the CCM. This is the case when you are alone driving down the highway, and all of a sudden your AW comes firing through because your LCM has nodded off to sleep or is distracted with steering your automobile. In most cases, of course, not wanting to lose your inspiration, you immediately begin scrambling for something to write or draw on. So, there will be no

"If you limit your choices only to what seems possible or reasonable, you disconnect yourself from what you truly want and all that is left is a compromise."
ROBERT FRITZ

more scrambling for pieces of paper, catching inspirations on the back of envelopes or shopping bags. All of this is possible only as long as you continually and consistently allow your CCM to make time for your AW, and especially the PAs who come with it.

Third, when plugged in to your AW and its PAs, you will have no idea where it is that you are going on a day-to-day basis.

This, as with the first appearance of your unknown or unrecognized PAs, may scare or concern you, all of which is addressed with a blanket solution in the next chapter. Just try to keep control of your reactions during this exciting time by keeping an eye on your breathing. Remember, if you can control your breathing, you can control your reactions and, thus, any inappropriate reactions as well.

Fourth, what you are experiencing is very natural.

Your AW, who may have been waiting on your CCM for decades, wants you to share your art even more than you may want to. So, it will do whatever it has to do to keep you going.

What that means is that your AW will initially offer you only one idea at a time to keep you from becoming overburdened. I know, for if you are anything like my typical student, you may feel as if your mind is overrun with ideas, inspirations, and purposes. However, the truth is that in the beginning your AW offers up only one idea through your CCM at a time. The reason that its offerings may appear to be more than one idea is because your AW, as desperate as it has become to grasp and capture your attention, will do whatever it can to get you to look its way, even

"Gardens are not made by singing 'Oh, how beautiful' and sitting in the shade."
RUDYARD KIPLING

if that means fragmenting its message in several different directions.

The reason that your AW does not release all that you will eventually need to know all at once is because it realizes that if it does so, you will lose interest in it and never follow through on the completion of your purpose. Think about it. If you went to a bookstore and purchased a novel, began reading it and 22 pages into it you realized exactly how everything was going to turn out, would you be interested in reading through until the end? Of course not.

Your AW knows this about you. So, if you only know as much as you need to know to complete that day's session, that is good. If you only know enough to complete the next page, paragraph, sentence, or word, that's even better. In fact, the less you are consciously aware of, the deeper your CCM connection with your AW.

Once your lead PA is fully flushed out, and I will cover how this happens shortly, he, she, or it will then lead you to and introduce you to another PA, who will eventually introduce you to another, who will then introduce himself, herself, or itself to you, before leading you to another.

This will continue on down the line until all of your PAs have been fully flushed out. The result of this entire experience becomes the understanding you need to trust these PAs to do the work for you.

Once this understanding has taken place, your PAs will begin meeting during your sessions, sometimes almost as a committee. As discussions are held, decisions are made about the direction and intent of what it is that they will

"He is not busy being born; he is busy dying."

BOB DYLAN

129

be doing, and what role each of them will play in it, and how the specific points that each embodies will be represented. This usually takes place during the *Living Outline* stage with the index cards in the next chapter. Once this is completed, then whatever you are to do for whatever reason begins taking off on its own and composes itself through your PAs.

A student of mine from Columbus, Ohio, an attorney by trade and a very logical person, was completely astounded by the unfolding of these events as they relayed themselves. Finally, her characters began to commune amongst themselves. From that point forward, with each call to me, she would begin with a chuckle and then say, "Well, they decided to..."

It is not unusual during this stage for your PAs, who definitely have their own minds and destinies, to change their positions, occasionally bring in a new member or to throw out an old one. The entire process functions very much like production meetings leading up to the successful conclusion of a major motion picture. These are always the big-ticket actors, guiding the wisdom of you, the director. With that comes much debate and rearranging. That is just how it works with you and your PAs.

UNDERSTANDING THE BACKGROUNDS OF YOUR PAS

Understanding the backgrounds and motivations of your PAs is essential because without this, you, or in this case your controling LCM, will not possess the trust necessary to allow your PAs to do what they have appeared to do.

Ponder that for a moment. Before you can trust someone, you first have to know that person. In human terms, that may mean just getting to know them through dating or hanging out, or whatever the needs of the type of relationship that you have entails. On the business end, you review resumes, call references, interview, and give trial runs on the job. All of this comes as the result of an effort to get to know and to eventually be able to trust the person entering your life. Understanding your PAs so that you will be able to trust them to do their job is no different.

The first component that one explores in either a personal or professional association is the sociological background of the person whom you are getting to know. Look at where they are from, what kind of family they were raised in, where they went to school, what they majored in, what their parents did for a living, what it is that they most aspire to do with their lives, and what steps they have taken to accomplish these goals, etc., etc. Ultimately, through all of the probing, you are looking to answer one question, "How has this person's past contributed to where he or she presently is in his or her life, and why?" The last part of that question, featuring the "why," is far and away the most important part. It is not enough in your questioning to simply come away with a stock answer. Remember, our LCMs seek understandings, which draw us to go beyond mere factual replies, into a much deeper appreciation of the inner workings of our PA's mind, soul, spirit, and life.

"I am in the present. I cannot know what tomorrow will bring forth. I can know only what the truth is for me today. That is what I am called upon to serve, and I serve it in all lucidity."
IGOR STRAVINSKY,
1936

After your PAs have offered you all of the necessary information your LCM needs to understand, they will lead you in the direction of their psychological makeups. In other words, your LCM will be shown "How what they have experienced in their lives has led them to who they are and to what they represent." Your LCM's understanding of them in this arena will enable you to affiliate with them. This is also from where your PA's motivating passions will come.

After your PAs have introduced you to their sociological and psychological backgrounds, they will exhibit for your LCM how these two basic components are reflected on a physical basis in their present lives. For example, were we to study Herman Melville's legendary character in *Moby Dick*, Captain Ahab, one physical factor of this severely angry man would stand out above the rest. That, of course, would be the man's wooden leg, the result of his last tussle with the great white whale, Moby Dick.

Each time that Ahab enters a scene, his leg continually reminds us of his motivating passion, which is his uncontrollable hatred for the whale. The presence of his peg leg is a continual reminder of that throughout the book. It also serves as a perfect example of how a character truly represents who he or she is by physically manifesting it in one form or another.

Another good example of this can be drawn from the movie *Rocky*. In the film, Rocky represents an exaggerated version of the "Have nots." How is that depicted? It is depicted through Rocky's life itself, where he lives, how he lives, how he dresses, how he talks. You get the idea. What is Rocky's goal? Rocky's goal is to be somebody, to leave behind all that has been physically manifested in his present life. Of course, in sequels, Rocky does eventually win often enough to be able to leave behind the physical representations of who he was. However, in *Rocky III*, he loses himself after being pummeled by Clubber Lang, played by Mr. T. Then it is only after he returns to his roots that he is able to rediscover his true strength as a fighter and as a man. That is how a PA will represent who he or she is to you and/or your LCM. The physical components of a PA are just tangible representations of the sociological and psychological components that make up each aspect of a PA.

What I have shared with you is simply a system for better understanding what will happen naturally when connecting with your PAs.

So where do PAs come from? They come from somewhere inside of you. Why are they surfacing now? So that your AW can help expose your CCM and LCM to them, so that you may understand them and, thus, grow beyond them. This, of course, is all taking place so that you may move farther and faster toward becoming as happy and as productive as possible.

A form of art becomes the key because it allows you to connect as directly with the Ultimate Source as possible. The methods that can be used to release this expression are endless. Picasso and Michelangelo chose painting, Bergman used films. Whatever or however you choose to release your AW is up to you. But it is now time for you to do so. Rest assured. Otherwise, you wouldn't be reading this book.

"Strong lives are motivated by dynamic purposes."
KENNETH HILDEBRAND

133

A LOOK BACK AND A LEAP FORWARD

"Wealth is not in making money, but in making the man while he is making the money."
JOHN WICKER

Step 1. Take the necessary steps to prepare yourself for this next adventure, and allow your mind to drift back to a very special, sacred place in your life. Everyone has one. Maybe yours was in your childhood bedroom, in your backyard, in a closet, outside your parents' house somewhere, maybe in a tree. Whatever, allow yourself to go there now, and back to the time when you last went there, and your reason for going there at that time. How was it that you felt at the time? Why were you there? What colors, sounds, temperature surrounded you at the time? Allow them all to come back to life so you can feel as if you were actually back there.

Remember to release any tension you may feel by blowing it out with your breath. Take a few moments just to let yourself go into whatever it was that you felt on that day and at that time.

Step 2. Then, out of nowhere, allow the presence of someone or something you don't know to appear next to you in the image in your mind. Stay with the experience, and don't allow your reactions to get the better part of you. Remember to breathe away any and all

134

tension that you may feel. Take as
many deep breaths as necessary and
blow them out, so that you may become
calm and accepting of this experience.

Step 3. Take a few moments to study the
image in front of you. What overwhelming feeling or impression do you
derive from this person's or this thing's
posture or general appearance? Is there
a smell that you sense from being
around this image or an all-providing
feeling?

Turn your focus to the face and then the eyes
of this individual. Drink in this person's eyes,
until you go beyond these "windows of the soul"
and directly to the very deepest part of this
being. Then, once there, look back out at yourself through the perspective of this individual.
From this entity's perspective, what do you see
of you? Remember to breathe out any tension
that you may be feeling at this time, and don't
move on to the next steps until you find yourself
perfectly calm and openly responsive.

Step 4. Allow yourself to drink in any and all
reflections of what this person sees and
thinks of you. Allow his or her thoughts
and feelings to become your own. Then
open your eyes and allow all that you
feel to be released openly onto the
paper before you.

If at any time you lose your connection or
your writing comes to a halt before 45 minutes of

*"It is the force of the ocean back
of the wave that gives the wave
its power."*
BAIRD T. SPALDING
*Life and Teaching of the
Masters of the Far East*

135

"From the universal consciousness we can draw all knowledge."

BAIRD T. SPALDING
Life and Teaching of the Masters of the Far East

time, close your eyes, take a few deep breaths, making sure to reconnect with your nostril breathing, and then connect once again with this individual, and his or her feelings, and begin writing again.

This is also a wonderful opportunity to practice reciprocal communication between you and the archetypes that appear in your mind. If at any time during this writing exercise or any exercise beyond this point, you have a question of any sort pop up in your mind, don't hesitate to ask the archetype for whatever it is that you may seek an answer to. After you do that, make sure to sit quietly as you await a reply, so that you may receive it.

CHAPTER SEVEN: LET THE CARDS DO THE TRICK

7

As discussed earlier, back when you were a baby or very young child, your CCM was allowed to be openly connected with your AW. If you were happy, you laughed. If you were sad, you cried, and if you were mad, you screamed, yelled, threw something. During those early years, your parents and other family members were your whole world, and they applauded however it was that you felt and whatever form it was that you chose to express it in.

However, as you got bigger and older, much of what was once appreciated in you and your CCM was no longer seen as acceptable. Over time, you were taught to think as opposed to feel. The older you got the more this foreign form of living was expected of you, and your LCM disproportionately evolved as the control-

"The imagination may be compared to Adam's dream – he awoke and found it truth."
KEATS

ling force in your life.

The first step in helping you make what was thought to be a necessary conversion came in the form of punishment or discipline for openly expressing the feelings of your AW through your CCM. Then eventually when you did choose to commune with some form of art, you found yourself trapped behind a logical barrier.

Eventually, a wall formed between your CCM and your LCM. This wall was constructed of the learned/conditioned, inappropriate responses to our AW. It was these knee-jerk responses that eventually separated you from your AW and the Ultimate Source and took you away from their natural, spontaneous expressions.

To get back to the point where the act of expressing can once again become the natural, AW/CCM-connected state it was meant to be, this wall needs to be removed. If it is not removed, you will never be any better, more productive, happier, or more successful than you have been up to this point. For each time you choose to follow the callings of your AW/CCM connection, you will have to climb that everheightening wall again and again.

This chapter is designed to remove that wall once and for all, so that you may live the expressive, peaceful, purposeful life that was meant for you.

"And God smiled again, and the rainbow appeared, and curled itself around his shoulder."
JAMES WELDON JOHNSON

138

WHAT ARE "THE CARDS" AND WHY DO THEY WORK?

By cards, I mean 3 x 5 index cards. My initial introduction to these powerful and useful tools came while I was knee-deep in my search for the 'absolute truths' concerning literary expression. During this phase of my development, I was reading every book on writing I could get my hands on. What I was looking for were the steps or methodology I was sure were available to make writing the breeze that it could be.

While reading through piles of books, I stumbled upon a recently released work by Syd Field, who has gone on to author several other books on writing screenplays, and is far and away the industry's most knowledgeable authority on the subject. In the course of reading his book, I discovered that Fields, an advocate of the 'inside/outside' approach to screenwriting, suggested that his readers use index cards to release the basic concepts of their screenplays.

I began pondering the significance of Field's suggestion and came to the conclusion that this method would work extremely well, not just with screenplays, but with any form of art. It wasn't long before I put his suggestion into play with my writing. So effective was this technique, that I have been employing it for the last two decades, not only with my own work, but also with that of my students.

When considering why these little gems are so effective and efficient, it is, first, important to remember that the unconditional AW connection

"That must be wonderful; I don't understand it at all."
MOLIERE,
1622

139

is both a freedom seeker and a giver of freedom. Thus it does not relate well to any limiting rules and/or restrictions. Instead, it prefers pages without lines that allow it to express openly and freely. Index cards provide that option, either by writing on the side without lines or through purchasing lineless cards.

Second, it is also absolutely essential to keep in mind that your often-exercised LCM, as opposed to your atrophied CCM, is still in control of your consciousness. What that means is that your LCM rides shotgun, monitoring your CCM's every move, action, thought, or decision.

Thank God, though, that the LCM, which is very inflexible, can be fooled or misled easily. The index cards become useful in that circumstance, because when we begin to release what our AW has to say on them, the LCM doesn't see us doing anything of value. All it believes we are doing is scribbling some useless little notes on small scraps of paper. Its authority is not being challenged, and so it feels safe and protected. Writing on index cards doesn't scare your LCM.

Third, the blockage or wall we seek to remove has been built one conditioned response at a time. So, to remove this wall, it needs to be taken down, one conditioned response at a time. To be able to achieve our ultimate goal, each emotion, which is tied to each conditioned response, needs to be identified, acknowledged, and expressed individually, given its own voice, and eventually its own form of release.

What this translates to, in the first of the three stages your work with the cards will take, is what I refer to as the *cathartic phase*.

"Everyone thinks of changing the world, but no one thinks of changing themselves."
TOLSTOY

PHASE ONE: THE CATHARTIC CLEANSING

This is the first stage of what you will experience as you begin your work with the cards.

Remember, what will happen will happen naturally and on its own as long as you follow the *Three Rs of Writing*. It is also important to keep in mind during this phase to release only one thought, feeling, or image onto each card, which in most cases translates to one word.

The reason that you are being asked to adhere to this is because the conditioned responses that currently make up the wall between you and your AW need to be given their own voice and opportunity to express what it is that they embody before they can fully be released.

You will be somewhat surprised, if not shocked, when you begin using the cards and entering into this phase. Thoughts and feelings, most of which you will have denied for years if not decades, will begin to express themselves. Since these cathartic expressions will have absolutely nothing to do with whatever it is that you may have felt that you wanted to express as your purpose, you will initially wonder why they are even appearing in the first place.

This phase signals the CCM's dropping of the wall, which exists between your LCM and it. Please be aware that if you fully give in to this process this one time and keep perfoming your art in one shape or another, this cathartic stage will never have to be repeated ever again. Your AW will see to that, as long as it is given a forum for its unadulterated expression through your CCM. The result of this phase is that your AW is

"But if a man happens to find himself he has a mansion which he can inhabit with dignity all the days of his life."
JAMES MICHENER

once again freed through your CCM back into your life, and you will never go back to being frightened or overcompromised ever again.

PHASE TWO - HELLO PAs

As the wall between you and your AW falls, room will be made for whatever it is that seeks to express itself through you. Contrary to the cathartic phase, you can express as much as you want on each card. You no longer have to limit yourself to one thought or feeling or image per card.

In each case, your PAs will eventually, totally, and completely appear as an image. In some cases, this image will be personified in the form of some sort of being. In other cases, your images will manifest in the form of strategic depictions of how the themes that will make up your work can and will be best expressed.

In either case, these images will continue to evolve and introduce themselves to you on "the cards" until all have been released and fully fleshed out, so that you may derive the proper understandings and, thus, the confidence to embrace the next phase.

PHASE THREE - THE LIVING OUTLINE

As your PAs step fully into your consciousness, bright, clear images of what it is that they will be writing with you will pop into your mind, until all of your writing on the cards becomes devoted to the relaying of what lies inside your AW connection. As with Phase Two, write as

"Joy is the feeling of grinning inside."
DR. MELBA COLGROVE

much per card as you would like.

Some of what will be released in this phase will astound you as the message you have been carrying around with you, with the cathartic wall now removed, begins to be released in outline form.

What a confidence builder it is to finally be introduced to the message or purpose that has been driving you all these years. Along these same lines, much of what you have received glimpses of over the years will finally begin to make sense as the pieces of this puzzle are finally given the opportunity to fall into place.

The whole idea behind this phase is to keep releasing whatever it is that has been trying to get out of you onto the cards until you no longer have anything new to say.

BEYOND PHASE THREE

At that point, stop writing on the cards, and go out and purchase the largest bulletin board that you can find and a few hundred tacks to go along with it.

Once you have done that, take the time you had designated to work with your cards each day, follow the preparatory steps to insure you are in an AW-connected state, and begin sorting your cards into three distinct sections:

1) *Cathartic Material*

2) *Releasing of PAs*

3) *Your Living Outline*

"The ancestor of every action is a thought."
EMERSON

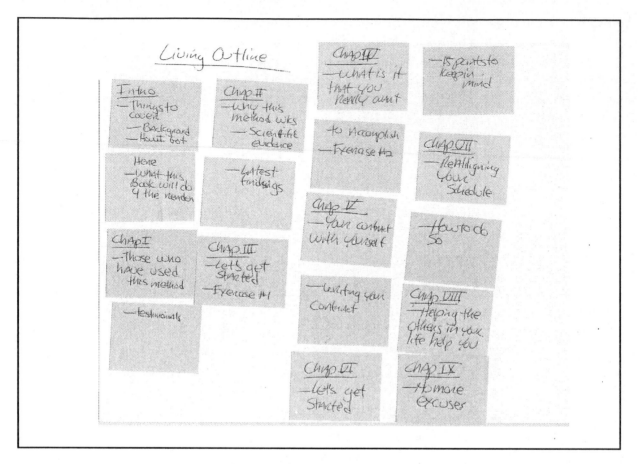

Living Outline example.

Set the cards for the first two sections aside and take the remaining cards for the *Living Outline* and begin tacking them in chronological order on your bulletin board. If you have so many cards that they don't all fit on one bulletin board, you may need to consolidate some of your comments down from several cards to one or two.

"Be not simply good; be good for something."
HENRY DAVID THOREAU

PUTTING THE CARDS INTO PLAY

I recently saw a greeting card that really grabbed my attention. On the outside cover was a three-stage photo of a young white dove, first jumping off a limb, opening its wings, and then taking flight. The inscription on the inside of the card simply read: "Sometimes all that is needed is a leap of faith." That is all you will need here as well; the cards, your CCM, and your AW will take care of the rest. What will happen as a result of this experience is that:

1. *The wall between you and your CCM and AW will be permanently removed.*

2. *You will reconnect or connect with your CCM, your AW, and your PAs.*

3. *Your PAs will release a blueprint version of your life-changing message or purpose.*

All of which will:

1. *Enable you to reconnect with your CCM and your AW;*

2. *Finally give you the confidence, connection, and insight to properly commit to that which you have felt drawn to for so long;*

3. *Form the foundation of whatever it is your living message may be.*

To successfully complete this step, you will need to purchase a minimum of 1,500 3 x 5 index cards. The cards which are unlined on both sides would be the best. However, if all you can find are those which are lined on one side, simply use the unlined side when writing with this drill.

I realize that the concept of the cards, all they represent, and all they do, is rather puzzling to your LCM. So, before moving on, I decided to include some further information on exactly how these little gems work.

As mentioned above, it's best if you can write first thing after awakening each day.

The hour that you initially set aside may seem like a great stretch for you. Don't worry though. Your concerns will all subside quickly in a day or two after the positively addictive tendencies of this method take over. This happens, of course, as the result of your addiction to the unconditional love from your AW that will come streaming through your CCM after the completion of the cathartic phase.

As mentioned earlier, you will go through three phases of development and release through your work with your cards. This will happen naturally and all on its own as long as you sim-

"Great minds have purposes, others have wishes."
WASHINGTON IRVING

ply show up, shut up, sit down, and write. Your CCM and AW will take care of the rest.

To best facilitate this step, follow the procedures that I have already shared on how to reach the desired AW connection.

Begin this step as soon as possible.

CINDI GAWNE AND "THE CARDS"

Because this entire procedure can prove mystifying to your LCM, I've included some reflections from one of my students, Cindi Gawne, as she moved through the cards. Even though your response to the cards may vary because of your chosen art form, in general, each student goes through the same exact three phases, just in his or her own way.

"As I walked out of the classroom at the University of Tennessee that warm April afternoon, I was determined to pursue my passion for writing, but even more so, I felt determined to have what I felt I saw in you that day – true contentment, joy, the 'I'm glad to be alive and love what I do' attitude, and the knowing that you had touched others made a difference, literally changed lives. Rekindled was my burning desire to empathize, encourage, and inspire hope to others – on paper and through my actions and attitude.

"I wanted to briefly share with you excerpts from my notes and writing assignments as described in the workshop, your book, and from

"Courage is doing what you're afraid to do. There can be no courage unless you're scared."
EDDIE RICKENBACKER

147

your website:

"The Cards" and "Tom was right..."

"4/28/02 2:30 a.m. – Notes from my first pack of 4 x 6 unlined index cards:

"This seems overwhelming when I see how many blank cards are left....want to stop writing and go to sleep, yet want to complete my goal....don't know that I've really said anything yet but keep writing what comes to mind....almost seems out of my control. Finally, the last stack of cards from the first pack, but now I don't want to stop! Card #99 of the first stack! Have written a lot, but don't see any story developing yet, but that's what Tom said is sup-posed to happen.

"Tom was right, writing on the cards is very helpful in self-examination and expression of pri-vate thoughts and fears....sure do ask myself a lot of questions, particularly, why?

"4/30/02 – Still filled with a lot of emotions and questions – not a whole lot of detail about a story coming out yet, but that's what Tom pre-dicted. He was right again, the more I write long-hand, the better and easier it is to read and still write with speed. Last card in today's stack – time to try another of Tom's ideas – acknowledge my accomplishment and go stand in the waves and watch the pelicans again.

"5/3/02 – I think doing cards is very helpful, but really want to start writing some kind of story. Tom said I would feel that way and he's on target again.

"5/5/02 – Very protective of MY CARDS! Dorito chip on chair and seagull wanted it – don't care as long as he doesn't peck at my cards.

"5/8/02 – When I ran out of things to say,

ideas for Lowell's story started flowing. Hey, Tom, I think my 'AW' is finally getting a chance to speak. It feels great!

"5/11/02 – Tom encouraged writing in the morning – not sure about that since I seem to be more nocturnal, but I do feel better and accomplished when writing first thing....get feelings out and no stress to finish them if tired or interrupted later....don't disappoint myself.

"5/14/02 – My writing sabbatical – Four days, just me, myself, and I. Heaviest yet, most important thing I had to haul upstairs were 'my cards.' First thing I thought of to do when I woke up this morning was start writing – didn't matter what ... just write... This is me – what feels comfortable and natural and of value – talking with my pen rather than my mouth.

"5/15/02 – Just like Tom predicted, I'm not writing as many index cards – not as many emotions to deal with. Actually started work on draft of short story instead... Tom, I LOVE these cards – with my personality, I don't know how I lived without them... Have cards, have pens, will travel.

"5/17/02 – Finished the drafts of 3 short stories – Tom was right (again) – this feels great! Must be feeling more confident with my writing because I'm asking more people to read it. Am very open, even eager for all comments – anything to improve. I think Tom mentioned that, too.

"Helpful Hints to Avoid Panic:

"I learned quickly that you need to stock your 'writing arsenal.' When minor panic set in when I only had 1/2 stack of cards left and so much to write! Furthermore, always have

"When one door of happiness closes, another opens, but often we look so long at the closed door that we do not see the one that has been opened for us."
HELEN KELLER

149

"I go on working for the same reason that a hen goes on laying eggs."

H. L. MENCKEN

enough pens so if one runs out of ink, which happened more quickly then I ever would have expected, I have a back up so I can keep writing.

"Another lesson I learned – Hold onto your cards when you stand up when sitting at the water's edge – luckily they floated in the salt water and dried without running or sticking together.

"The Big, Blank, White Sheet Of Paper:

"Writing on cards is OK, to start writing on this paper, daunting!

"Few days later... Thinking of writing on large paper still intimidating, yet beginning to seem challenging and exhilarating.

"Want so much to write on big paper – think maybe I'll feel like a 'real writer,' but keep putting it off.

"First used paper; wrote my 'I choose...list' – not so scary.

"Actually liked writing on large drawing pad. Makes me feel like an artist, like actually creating something. When reviewing it later, do 'touch ups' with red pen. Will have finished product, unique to any other."

Chapter Eight: Consistently Reinforce Your AW's Purpose

The simple truth is that all your LCM has been exposed to up to this point has had a distinct effect on you. The sheer repetition of these influences has caused it to associate pleasure with the denial of your AW/CCM connection and pain with anything having to do with it.

Just consider how artists, those supposedly with the connection, are depicted in movies or in books. Is there ever a sane one? Almost all are either broke, afflicted with some sort of sexual disease and/or addiction, or under intense pressure to meet an impossible deadline.

Of course, this form of erroneous characterization has made for wonderful copy for centuries. But it has done tremendous damage to your willingness to connect with your AW/CCM.

The real truth, of course, is all around us.

"Paradise is where I am."
VOLTAIRE

Persons such as bestselling author John Grisham were able to break through all of the dogma and succeed not only financially but retain their personal virtues.

Grisham was a struggling attorney with no formal training in writing before opening up to his CCM and listening to his AW paid off in hundreds of millions of sales that led him to become the literary voice of America.

What was Stephen King before following his AW/CCM connection that led him away from his jobs as a janitor, convenience store clerk, and onto the bestseller list for the last twenty years plus?

Andrew Greeley was a priest.

Tom Clancy was in business.

Anthony Robbins was too young and didn't even have a real job yet. In fact, very rarely do you find a successful artist who is a direct byproduct of the societal and educational system, which has unknowingly strived so hard to steer us away from our true selves.

"The most difficult people that I have to work with are those with Ph.D.s," claims award-winning New York Editor Michael Seidman. "They focus way too much on the rules, instead of the heart and how the rules can work for the heart."

The personal arena is oftentimes nearly as critical as the artistic.

"No one all of a sudden becomes a successful artist at your age."

"But why would you want to do that?"

"Why don't you just take a class in the arts or something to cure this ridiculous urge of

"Destiny is not a matter of chance, it is a matter of choice; it is not a thing to be waited for, it is a thing to be achieved."
WILLIAM JENNINGS BRYAN

yours? You're no artist, honey. You're a housewife and you have children and Bob to take care of. Isn't that enough? Why would you even want to pursue some silly art and risk losing all that?"

"What you did was really nice, and I'm really proud of you for doing so well. But you're so young. I just don't think that anyone is really going to take you seriously. Plus, I don't really think there is a future in it. Why don't you put that wonderful mind of yours to work in something with a better future associated with it? Then, when you've gotten your degrees and you have a little spare time, you can take up your art as a hobby."

"You want to do what? But how are you going to make a living?"

The last one especially gets to me. Do you know that I have been authoring books for nearly two decades now, and yet when people first meet me they still say to me – "Ah, so you write books; how do you make a living then?" The odd circumstance about all of this is that in the vast majority of cases, the AW-connected activities that they have run away from, and to which I have directed my life, have brought so much more to my life, including financial gain, than they have yet to experience in theirs.

How they react, though, is not their fault. They, like you, to one degree or another, have just been taught to associate writing with deprivation and pain. Even though the evidence contrary to that is all around them, they cannot see

"Here is the test to find whether your mission on earth is finished: If you're alive, it isn't."
RICHARD BACH

153

it because of how they have been conditioned to view the situation. This string of knee-jerk responses is also what has held you back from pouring yourself into your artistic outlet. Now it's time to change all that.

IT ONLY RECOGNIZES ASSOCIATIONS WITH PAIN AND PLEASURE

As much of a deterrent as they have become, as mentioned, our LCMs are actually very much on our sides.

Since its main purpose is to keep us away from pain, it naturally leads us away from our art since it associates it with displeasure.

What the LCM has been taught is at the base of that constant struggle that's continually raging inside all of us. Our CCMs are continually leading us to the expression of our feelings, while our LCMs are constantly pulling us off in the opposite direction.

However, what do you think would happen if you suddenly took a deliberate step to begin associating pleasure with your art? What do you think would happen? What would that do to the constant inner struggle that is at work in all of us? What would it do for your CCM and for you as a result?

The sky would then once again be the limit, just like when you were a child. But you would have the wisdom of a fully grown adult to finally take advantage of the situation. Suddenly, the

"My choice early in life was either to be a piano player in a whorehouse or a politician. And to tell the truth, there's hardly any difference."
HARRY S. TRUMAN

personal barriers would be gone – poof! And our strongest adversary would instantly become our most staunch ally.

THE TWO STEPS

Two steps are necessary to change any result in your life. Congratulations. You have already taken the first one by transforming a desire into an action by acquiring this book.

It is the second step that now needs to be put into play. That step deals with getting your LCM to reassociate your art with pleasure. To be able to succeed at this step, it is essential that you be open and honest with the following exercise. I have found that the best way to do so is just to have fun with it.

"Blessed is the man who has found his work."
ELBERT HUBBARD

"I CHOOSES"

Step 1. Find as large a blank, lineless piece of paper as you can. Even if all you have is an 8.5 x 11 piece of copy paper, that will do fine.

Step 2. Follow the steps from earlier in this book into an AW-connected state.

Step 3. While there, allow the reflection of who you were, where you were, and any significant conditions surrounding the time when you were last most expressive. Once in that place, take several deep breaths, relax, and spend a few moments just communing with the reflections of yourself in the image, and how it was that you felt.

Step 4. Then see the words "I choose" superimposed over the scene in your mind. Blow out any tension. Then take a moment to allow thoughts and feelings to flow into your mind in response to the words "I choose."

Step 5. Open your eyes, pick up your pen and write "I choose" anywhere on your piece of paper, and allow whatever response you feel to flow out. Then quickly write down "I choose" again, and allow whatever it is that you feel to flow out. Repeat this again and again and again and again, going to a second and third page and a fourth page if you need to until you can write down "I choose" and nothing else comes out.

"It is the supreme act of the teacher to awaken joy in creative expression and knowledge."
ALBERT EINSTEIN

I have accomplished more than I would have ever hoped to in the past two weeks and have successfully thrown out 'overwhelming' from my vocabulary. I am me. Stronger than ever, and I love it."

KAREN
Student, Florida

I choose to be happy rather than sad
I choose to be honest rather than a liar
I choose the light over the dark
I choose to be me, no matter what the cost it's the only way to be
I choose love over hate
I choose to love what I do.
I choose to do only what I love
I choose happiness
I choose joy
I choose to be thankful
I choose to see a reason for everything
I choose what I believe to be the Universal Law
I choose to run rather than to walk
I choose to climb rather than to fall
I choose to do what it is that I feel called to do with my life
I choose health over fear
I choose anything, any alternative over fear
I choose to use fear as a challenge, an opportunity
I choose bravery over fear
I choose potential pain over fear
I choose to live, really live, every minute, every moment at the cutting edge
    of expression
I choose to cheer rather than boo
I choose to be a good and faithful friend
I choose the company of those who know how to love over any others
I choose to be alone, by myself, rather than being lonely in the presence
    of another
I choose to celebrate as opposed to grubling and grieving
I choose to live where I want and to do what I love to do
I choose to believe in love and the love of my life
I choose to be a light in the face of darkness
I choose to explore, uncover, and discover me
I choose to share that "me" with the world in whatever shape or form
    it takes
I choose to appreciate myself for whatever I am whenever I am
I choose to love
I choose to love me

Example of the "I Choose" exercise

Step 6.   Then use the words, "I choose to have," in place of "I choose" and do the exercise over again.

HE GAINED TWELVE POUNDS

A number of years ago, a student of mine from Richmond, Virginia, was having a challenging time getting into a CCM/AW-connected state.

To relieve him of his struggle, I prescribed the aforementioned exercise. I then told him to divide his responses to his *"I choose"* and *"I choose to have"* into three categories: small, medium, and large desires. I then told him to choose one item off the small list each time he completed his daily writing assignment.

Immediately, his writing output skyrocketed. After a few weeks' exposure to this new tool, I asked him to give me an assessment of how his work with his writing was going.

"I never wrote like this before," he stated enthusiastically. "The words are just flowing out of me. I have also found it so much easier to approach my writing each day. There is so much less of a barrier. In fact, I feel as if I have been able to move beyond whatever barriers were there to a point where I now feel completely drawn to write, no matter how it is that I am feeling physically or emotionally.

"There is only one bad thing though," he continued.

"What's that?" I asked, somewhat surprised.

"I've gained twelve pounds."

"Twelve pounds?" I questioned.

Well, what he didn't tell me was that he was

using Snickers candy bars as his daily reinforcement. He also didn't inform me that the Snickers bar he chose to use each day was one of those giant ones, the type you find at truck stops that take two hands to carry back to your vehicle. No wonder he put on so much weight.

I couldn't convince him to stop using Snickers as his chosen form of behavior modification, but I did get him to downshift to the bite-size bar instead of the gigantic one. He eventually dropped the extra weight, kept the writing style and speed, and all was well that ended well.

YOU CAN GAIN, TOO

Now that you have got your list, break it into the three separate categories mentioned previously: small, medium, and large reinforcements.

Here's where the consistency comes in. Each day after you have completed one of the following art assignments, choose something off of the small list to offer yourself as a reward. Or up until that time, any time that you read or work with this book, choose something off of the small list. Use the medium list for reinforcing more extensive accomplishments, such as the completion of one of the major steps which follow. The last category is, of course, reserved for the completion of your rough and finished drafts, or for dealing with any major step taken toward your life's purpose, all of which will be completed by the end of this book.

It is very important that you give these reinforcements directly to yourself. The reason for this is twofold.

"The transformation of your world will depend on your remembering."
NEALE DONALD WALSCH
Communion With God

First of all, expecting others to do for you what they may not even be able to do for themselves, or to reward you for doing something that they don't understand is unfair.

Second, as you may already be beginning to understand, much of what you are and will be dealing with in this book bespeaks of learning to relove a certain, essential aspect of yourself, our CCM/AW connection, or your Ultimate Source self. So, it is important that it is you in charge here. For no one else, no matter how hard they try, can supplement what it is that you need to do for yourself.

You will not believe the jump in your production and confidence that this technique will offer you. One student that I had worked with and who had struggled something fierce to complete the draft of her first book was named Isabella.

"Isabella," I sternly reminded her, "you have worked very, very hard to complete the writing of your work. Now, it is very important that you make sure to give yourself a big reward as an acknowledgment of your accomplishment. Doing this, of course, is essential for you to begin accepting yourself as the author you are. So don't call me back until you have chosen something off your large list and have taken the necessary steps to give whatever it is that you have chosen to yourself. Do you understand?"

"Yes," she replied.

"Okay, good. Now, by the time we speak again, I expect you to have taken this step. Okay?"

"Yes."

Isabella called me back a week later, and I immediately asked her if she had done as I had

"The world is charged with the grandeur of God."
GERARD MANLEY
HOPKINS

160

instructed, to which she replied that she had.

I assumed that she had, indeed, done something special, but I was feeling nosy. I wanted to know what she had done for herself. Assuming that she had bought herself a new coat, taken herself away for a weekend, or whatever, I asked, "What was it that you did for yourself, Isabella?"

"Well, there was always this gorgeous little country cottage in England that I had always adored. So I made some calls, found the owner's name and number, and I bought it for myself over the phone."

Isabella is still writing, even today.

NEGATORY STUFF

If you follow the above procedures, there's no need for any separate form of negative reinforcement. Simply offer yourself something off one of your lists, if you have accomplished your desired writing task. Withholding what you have grown to appreciate will be enough for your LCM to begin screaming, "Hey, we have to paint, sculpt, sing, whatever today. When we do our art, we get that luscious cup of coffee, glass of wine, or savory piece of chocolate. So, let's do whatever it is that we have to do to get our person to do our art. You know, this art is a good thing, because it brings us good things. So, we need to keep doing it."

What a welcome change that will be!

"Every good thought you think is contributing its share to the ultimate result of your life."
GRENVILLE KLEISER

CHAPTER NINE: EXPOSING YOURSELF TO THE ART OF OTHERS

9

Connecting to your AW is invigorating. It is this connection that teaches you about yourself, life, and what you are here to do. It is this connection that makes you feel loved. So powerful is this release that the simple act of connecting with it becomes positively addicting. What that translates to is that your art, like any other addiction, eventually becomes nearly impossible to walk away from.

This form of an addiction is positive because it feeds your life and the desire of your soul. It is what you derive from this connection that keeps you coming back, even after dozens of years have passed.

It is this same positively addictive connection that brings you to the art of others. It's these artists whom you vicariously live through

Man: Do you belong here?
Fonzie: I belong everywhere.
HAPPY DAYS

when you are NOT in direct connection with your own AW.

However, there is also only one activity in which you could participate during the initial stages of communing with your art that could misdirect or prohibit it and that is studying or reviewing the art of other artists with a similar calling. Notice that I said 'initial.' There is no doubt that I am a committed advocate to the many benefits of studying another's work and learning from it. However, when you do this during the initial stages of getting into your own art, it severely stunts and potentially halts your transformation.

For when you do so, you connect to the CCMs and AWs of other artists. When you put a temporary moratorium on your review of the art of others and begin connecting with your own AW, the necessary space for your LCM to hear, feel, experience, and exclusively get to know your own AW/CCM-connected voice will be created.

In my estimation, for your LCM to get to fully know this side of yourself takes a good 30-90 days. After that, you can study the work of as many artists as you would like, as often as you would like, and it won't take your zest and desire away from your own connective experience.

From that time forward, doing so will directly benefit your own art. Before then, however, will severely damage your process. This becomes absolutely essential. For up until this time your LCM, who is unfamiliar with this voice of yours, will reject it. However, once it gets to know it, it will enthusiastically embrace it, just like it does with the voices of other artists with whom it has become familiar.

"We can secure other people's approval, if we do right and try hard; but our own is worth a hundred of it."

MARK TWAIN

CATHARTIC STAGE

In your work with the cards, you should be beyond both the cathartic phase and through with the release of the PAs. What this means is that at least 70 percent of the index cards you are filling should be focusing on your archetypes. If this is not the case, pick up the speed.

Also, if your Living Outline is not yet beginning to expose itself, there is an excellent chance that you may be pondering and thinking a bit too much, as opposed to just letting the emotion of your AW connection fly through your CCM.

If this happens to be the case, give in to the experience more, and pick up your speed so that you may more rapidly proceed to your third stage of development.

———————— ❧ ————————

"To express that which God has conceived for him should be man's great purpose in life."
BAIRD T. SPALDING
Life and Teaching of the Masters of the Far East

CHAPTER TEN: COMMITMENT

Contrary to what you may have been told, you don't lack commitment. In fact, you are very committed. Like so many others who are drawn to their true purposes, you have held down jobs, paid off loans, graduated from schools, and possibly even successfully raised children. Yet you have not given up on your purpose, and, most importantly, you have made time to do something about it. Bravo!

No, you are very brave and very committed. From my perspective, you don't have to commit more. You simply need to commit more wisely. What that means is committing to the following:

"The most important thing is to be whatever you are without shame."

ROD STEIGER

THE CONTRACT

There is one common denominator amongst all of the commitments you have followed through on. That common denominator is an agreement that you have entered into in some form with yourself and most probably an outside source or two as well. The presence of this formal or informal agreement directly led to the eventual accomplishment of whatever your chosen task happened to be.

In my work, with both myself and my students, I have found that a signed contract or an agreement is almost always the difference between success and failure.

Creating a contract such as this logistically will be the simplest step that you will be asked to take. You can write it in longhand, type it out, whatever, as long as it is committed to paper, copied, and distributed in the manner suggested. All of this, including mailing it, will cost you less than five dollars and take you less than an hour, travel time included.

The reason that it often takes so long to complete this necessary step, though, is because it is emotionally challenging.

Most of you have been talking about what you were going to do with your life for years. Your LCM has listened to all of your empty, verbal claims and nothing of substance has been completed. As a result, your LCM doesn't believe you when you say you're going to do whatever with your art. Can you blame it? In response, it needs something much more tangible to believe that you are actually going to take serious action. It

"There is no time like the pleasant."
OLIVER HERFORD

needs to see your commitment on paper.

Back when I was struggling with the release of my own AW, I was searching high and low for a solution that would enable me to become the author I already felt myself to be. It was then that a colleague of mine, a well-known sports writer named Dick Young, suggested that "I just write." Having run out of more convenient and less challenging alternatives, I finally decided to accept Dick's advice a few weeks later. Upon doing so, I laid out a production pace for myself to write daily for six months. Every day, the number of words that I wrote would grow until I was writing 7,000 words a day. In actuality, by doing so, I was admitting my desire to my LCM.

In a result I directly tie to this act, by the end of my six months, I had completed my first book, while working a job where I put in over 90 hours a week. During that time, I also landed the finest literary representative in the country who sold my book to the third largest publisher in the world a few weeks later. The sale enabled me to resign from my job with over three years' salary in the bank.

Until that point, I was like so many others. I had taken the classes, read all of the books, and talked incessantly about my goal, but I hadn't put it all on the line, turned it over to, and committed it to that author of that longtime desire in me – my AW.

Even today, I follow the same procedures any time that I write a book. I break the composition and completion of the blessed task into the stages, and then commit to them in writing. The rest takes care of itself.

I do the same with my students. In fact, I

"The great thing in this world is not so much where we are, but in what direction we are moving."

OLIVER WENDELL
HOLMES

will not work with a student who refuses to commit, in writing, to their own success. By not committing to and guiding and releasing their own success in writing, they are admitting to an unreadiness and an unwillingness. It's obviously not yet their time.

It is a common belief in many circles that a person doesn't make the necessary changes in his or her life until the pain has gotten so great that they finally have to make alterations and overcome their fears.

When I first began individually mentoring students on writing their books and screenplays, I did so purely on a scholarship basis. However, I had to stop doing so after a few months. Those students with whom I was working drained me emotionally. They were all excuses and no writing. It was then that I realized the mistake I had made was that I had not made them commit, in writing, to their intentions. My pain and suffering came to an abrupt halt after that, when I refused to take on any students who would not commit, in writing, to their work. The difference between those who committed in writing and those who did not was astounding.

The most daunting task I face as a mentor is to get my students to actually commit to their own success. As part of each of my classes, I invite the attendees to cement their commitments by sending me a copy of their agreement, sort of a formal rite of passage. Those who send me a contract stand a very high chance of connecting with their purposes and living their dreams. Those who are not ready to enter into a contract are not, and may not ever be, ready to experience success. Many of the latter group end

"When the truth has been nurtured within you, it asserts itself clearly in your life."
NEALE DONALD WALSCH
Communion With God

up retaking my class at some point down the road, or just wind up living vicariously through the lives, dreams, and expressions of others. That is how important this step is for you. Do it and you will in all likelihood succeed. Avoid it and in all likelihood, you won't.

BEFORE THE CONTRACT

Before moving forward with the specifics of the contract, it is important to generate as much enthusiasm for doing so as possible. It is also best that this enthusiasm be based upon understanding, confidence, vision, trust, and faith. Otherwise, it will wear off as quickly as the pregame hype football players have, until they suffer their first on-field hit.

To generate the reckless abandon and enthusiasm of your AW, it is important that you will have worked with your cards all the way through the third phase, where the *Living Outline* has been released and tacked up on your bulletin board.

The successful completion of the *Living Outline* will significantly lessen the struggle for your LCM. Once your outline is done, not only will your LCM finally begin to back off, but you will simply believe in the process so much more. It will just make taking the contract step so much easier. So, if you haven't already done so, complete the final phase of your work with the cards before moving on to the next section.

"Surrender does not transform what is, at least not directly. Surrender transforms you. When you are transformed, your whole world is transformed because the world is only a reflection."

ECKHART TOLLE
The Power of Now

171

YOUR WRITTEN COMMITMENT – SIGNED AND DATED

Even though some of the following contracts relate to the completion of books, please keep in mind that this essential step is necessary for whatever it is that your life purpose happens to be. I have simply included some contracts for aspiring writers because that is my area of expertise. As you will see, each one of the agreements is signed and dated. Your agreement needs to be signed and dated as well.

Your contract should convey as much passion as possible, for it is this passion that your LCM will especially feed off of as it gets behind you. The more excited it is, the more momentum it will generate for you.

GENERAL STATEMENT OF PURPOSE

Every agreement, no matter how small or large, has to have a general statement of purpose. This statement basically answers the question, "What is it that you are promising to do?"

If you are going to write a book or screenplay, state that. If you are going to do something much different, state that too. The time which you are allotting to complete your challenge should be addressed as well.

First, in calculating a livable time frame, many components need to be taken into consideration.

Second, I would strongly recommend that you not take into consideration what you have heard from sources outside of this program.

"When you cease to make a contribution then you begin to die."
ELEANOR ROOSEVELT

Third, I strongly suggest that you stay away from thinking about what is possible, and instead focus more strongly on what you believe would be possible after some alterations in your typical routine.

TIME FRAME

Speed is a very important component to consider. The faster that you perform your art, the less time you have to 'think.'

What speed does that translate to? On a weekly basis, eventually working two hours a day, six days a week. At that pace, as long as you remain connected to your AW, you should be able to complete the rough draft of whatever major project it is that you are working on, including something as lengthy as a book, in no more than five weeks.

In coming up with a more exact figure for yourself, simply compute the percentage of the eventual art form completed in a two-hour period. What is the average percentage completed? With books, for example, this would translate to the number of words composed and what percentage of the eventual finished outcome this would compose. How many sessions will it then take for you to fully finish the rough draft of your work?

"When a fantasy turns you on, you're obligated to God and nature to start doing it – right away."
STEWART BRAND

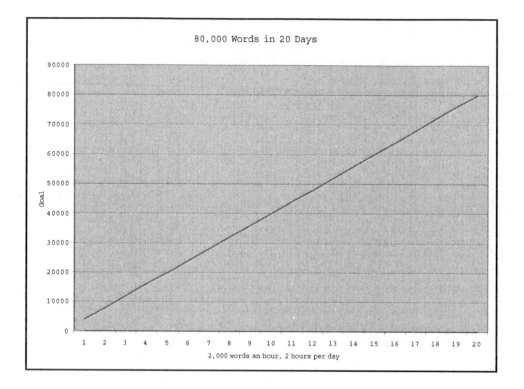

*Graph showing writing sessions at 2,000 words
an hour – 2 hours per day.*

THE WAGER

It is essential to keep in mind that an agreement of any sort is also a wager with yourself and, potentially, others. You are awarded with positive reinforcements upon the successful completion of your agreement. The opposite is true, of course, if your chosen task is not successfully completed in a timely fashion.

It is the correct balance between the positive and the negative, both of which are equally important catalysts, that offers you the best opportunity to reach your goal.

After you complete your agreement, make seven copies of it. Keep the first copy for yourself and insure that this document is in open view each and every time you do whatever it is that you will need to do to fulfill your purpose.

Send the second copy to me. Why? Because this announces your formal rite of passage. When I receive the contract, I will drop you a line in response.

If you don't already have my mailing address, it is: P.O. Box 4306, Sedona, AZ 86340. You can also fax me at 928/203-0264 or e-mail me through my website at www.ambassu.com.

There have been many influences that have carried you to this point, and not all of them have been pleasant. However, the truth is that your LCM, which this contract is being written for, is still motivated by the pressure of avoiding failure. There are persons who tangibly represent this potential failure in your life. There always have been. You know the ones I am referring to. The aunt, uncle, friend, colleague, sibling, or even parent who continually told you,

"No matter where your life takes you, no matter how far you stray from the path, you cannot extinguish the spark of divinity within your own consciousness. It was and is God's gift to you."
PAUL FERRINI
Reflections of the Christ Mind

against the calling of your own heart, that you couldn't do what you wanted to do with your art. In an odd and uncomfortable way, each of these persons have contributed to your success. They are now just about to make their largest and most significant positive contribution when you send three of these persons a copy of your agreement.

I realize this may seem ludicrous to you. However, there will be days when you will not be at your best, and during which time you will not feel like following through on your appointed task. It is during these stretches that you will need these people the most. For it is the fear associated with having to admit to them that you failed that will drive your LCM to get you back on and keep you on track.

The last two copies of your agreement are to be sent to two persons who love you unconditionally.

With each and every agreement that you send out, it is paramount that you make a promise to each person. Promise to give them something or to give up something that you would hate to lose if you do not complete, in a timely manner, your work of art, or any of the steps listed in your contract.

YOU NEED TO BE COMMITTED TO DO ANY GOOD

There are obviously many misnomers associated with living one's purpose. One of the most ridiculous is the misnomer that states you have

"Inspiration is the act of drawing up a chair to the writing desk."

ANONYMOUS

176

to be disciplined to be a success.

Frankly, as I mentioned before, you only need to be disciplined if you are either doing something that you don't like or if you are attempting to do something that you are frightened to do.

By the very fact that you have arrived this far into this book, I assume that for one reason or another that living your purpose is something you like or want to do. So the first case for discipline is already negated.

In regard to being frightened to live your purpose, the truth is that you will always be frightened to do so unless time is taken to reassociate doing so with pleasure. Once that step is taken, not only will you find it so much easier to do, but you will do it much better, and much more successfully as a result.

All that, of course, has already been addressed through your proper employment of reinforcement.

"Whether you think you can, or that you can't, you are usually right."

HENRY FORD

SAMPLE
CONTRACTS

INDIVIDUAL CONTRACT #1

On this seventh (7th) day of October in the year 2003, I (Author), do enter into this contract willingly and with full knowledge of what is expected of me by me. I write this contract in order to commit myself to writing a book, a book that is presently inside of me now. I will complete this book by Thanksgiving of the year 2003. I do understand the necessity of this contract binding me to a commitment of writing.

I will reserve two hours daily, six days a week, to write.

I will remove all distractions. I will set boundaries for those near and dear to me and ask them to respect those boundaries, so that I may have uninterrupted time.

I will do relaxing exercises before writing, while writing, and after writing.

I will allow my thoughts and feelings to flow freely onto blank index cards.

I will post my results on a bulletin board on the wall above my desk.

I will make a list of all that I would like to have and do.

I will break them into daily, weekly actions.

On a daily basis, I will reward myself with a cigarette and O'Doules, (even if it is 10 o'clock in the morning) on the patio.

When I have made a completion of one step, I will treat myself and my children to a full-course lobster meal at a restaurant.

When I have finished my final copy and have sent it off to the Literary Agent, I will travel to Sedona and spend the day, complete with a picnic lunch of my favorite foods, on the back site of Oak Creek Canyon. I will take pictures and rejoice in my favorite place. I will take my son and daughter, if possible.

I gladly and willingly and most excitedly do sign this contract.

_____   _____
Author   Date

INDIVIDUAL CONTRACT #2

On this day of November 24, 2003, I hereby openly make clear my intentions to finally complete the oil painting that I have partially sketched on canvas, and which has been keeping me up for years, and to start on my heartfelt career as a self-supporting artist.

My plan of action will be this:

A) I will rise every morning ninety minutes before I usually get up, follow *The Three Rs of Writing* to put me in the proper mood, and then paint.

B) By doing this, I plan to have my first painting completely finished by January 24, 2004.

C) By no later than January 25, 2004, I will begin individually contacting local galleries to find a place for it to be displayed. At that time, I will also contact galleries in other locales through the Internet. I will contact no less than one gallery a day, six days a week. I will stay with this routine for the sale of future works as well.

D) With this plan in mind, I will land the proper home for the painting by no later than February 27, 2004.

E) Any revenues raised from the sale of my first painting, or any that follow, will be placed in a special bank account established for the sole purpose of accumulating enough money for me to resign from my position at the bank and go to work at this full time.

F) As far as my routine and painting are concerned, I will stick with the aforementioned routine six days a week, each morning – moving from painting to painting – until I have earned enough to resign from my position. At that time, I will then follow the same routine with the *Three Rs of Writing* and devote myself to painting a minimum of five hours a day, with time put aside each day for the sales of my work.

I realize the importance of each person to whom I have sent a copy of this contract, and I call upon each one to police my heartfelt efforts in whatever way he or she chooses. If at any time I fall short of any of the goals listed above, and their corresponding deadlines, I hereby promise to treat each person who received a copy of this contract to a dinner at his or her favorite restaurant.

God is with us all.

Bert Zimpa

181

INDIVIDUAL CONTRACT #3

July 7, 2003 – I, Jan Smith, will begin following the dream of owning my own flower shop.

To make this dream happen, I will faithfully stay connected to my deepest inspiration by following *The Three Rs of Writing* and writing each morning for an hour.

The information that I gather from these sessions, I will use to guide me spiritually, financially, and logistically.

By no later than August 7, 2003, I will have chosen a general locale for the store.

By August 17, 2003, I will have contacted the SBA and set up a meeting with a counselor to help me put together the necessary plan to get a loan to finance my dream.

By working with the SBA and writing on the plan each morning, after following *The Three Rs of Writing*, I will have the business plan completed and ready for submission to loan counselors no later than October 10, 2003.

I will continue to follow my routine with my morning writing, and reserve time each day as well to make whatever adjustments or answer any questions that may arise and/or may be necessary in regard to the business plan.

By December 10, 2003, I will expect to have gained the necessary approval on a loan, and I will do whatever is necessary to dive into my life's work, with my own flower shop, by February 1, 2004.

To this goal, I devote all my heart and soul. May the results which are achieved become a reminder to many that our dreams come true. All that is needed is a little faith, consistent effort, and, most of all, that ultimate of all connections flowing through our life each day.

For each of you who has been chosen to receive a copy of this contract, you have carte blanche to check on my progress, per the above dates and terms, whenever you see fit. If I am caught falling behind on any, I will gladly donate one free hour of yard work to each and every one of you receiving this agreement.

May God guide all of our actions.

Jan Smith

INTENSIVE WRITER PROGRAM AGREEMENT #1

Tom Bird and Author_____ whose address is
_____ hereby agree to as follows:

Intensive Writing Program

A. Services to Be Rendered – Consultation and Review:

1. Mr. Bird shall provide an average of 4 consultations per week, specifically designed to lead and guide the author to the successful completion and revision of his or her books, during the period from _____ to _____.

2. Mr. Bird shall, upon completion, review the draft of the Author's one manuscript (one maximum) for the specific purpose of refining it for publication. The manuscript will be reviewed and commented upon no more than twice.

3. Once the author's manuscript is in a fully completed and finished form, Mr. Bird shall: assist the author in the composition of his or her query letter package; all components of his or her submission package to be submitted to prospective literary agents; provide a listing of literary agents and consult with the author on the choice of prospective literary agents; consult with the author on any suggestions or rewrite marketing strategies suggested by prospective literary agents; and serve as a marketing liaison between the author and the author's publisher, aggressively pursuing the goal of obtaining an appropriate publisher for the author's work.

B. Compensation

Mr. Bird shall be paid a non-refundable fee of ($_____).

If Mr. Bird chooses to allow payments, 25% of the above fee shall be due immediately, with the remaining payments divided over no more than the following two months, with each payment coming due on the _____ of each month, and the total amount paid in full no later than _____. If any of the aforementioned payments are received more than 10 days after the due date, a 10% late fee will be paid by the author.

If the author cancels out of this agreement before its completion, Mr. Bird will immediately be due his entire fee.

C. Other

If the author chooses to continue to consult with Mr. Bird after the conclusion of the consultation period set forth above, such further participation and consultation, both as to how and for how long, will be negotiated separately.

D. Default

All costs, attorneys' fees, and other expenses of enforcing this agreement shall be paid to the prevailing party by the losers, including collection fees and costs.

Acknowledged and agreed to by:

_____ _____
Author   Thomas J. Bird

_____ _____
Date   Date

INTENSIVE WRITER PROGRAM AGREEMENT #2

Tom Bird and Author,_____whose address is: _____ hereby agree to as follows:

Intensive Writing Program

A. Services to Be Rendered – Consultation and Review:

1. Mr. Bird shall provide an average of 4 consultations per week, specifically designed to lead and guide the author to the successful completion and revision of his or her books during the period from _____ to _____.

2. Mr. Bird shall, upon completion, review the draft of the Author's two manuscripts (two maximum) for the specific purpose of refining them for publication. Each manuscript will be reviewed and commented upon no more than twice each.

3. Once the author's manuscript(s) is/are in a fully completed and finished form, Mr. Bird shall: assist the author in the composition of his or her query letter package; all components of his or her submission package to be submitted to prospective literary agents; provide a listing of literary agents and consult with the author on the choice of prospective literary agents; consult with the author on any suggestions or rewrite marketing strategies suggested by prospective literary agents; and serve as a marketing liaison between the author and the author's publisher, aggressively pursuing the goal of obtaining an appropriate publisher for the author's work.

B. Compensation

In addition to the commission set forth below, Mr. Bird shall be paid a non-refundable fee of ($_____), which comprises a reduction from $_____, which would comprise Mr. Bird's regular fee for such a service.

If Mr. Bird chooses to allow payments, 25% of the above fee ($_____) shall be due immediately with the remaining payments divided over no more than the following five months, with each payment of ($_____) coming due on the _____of each month, and the total amount paid in full no later than _____. If any of the aforementioned payments are received more than 10 days after the due date, a 10% late fee will be paid by the author.

In consideration of lowering of Mr. Bird's regular fee, Mr. Bird shall be entitled to a commission on the amounts received by author as to said publication, which shall be as follows:

(a) First Book: A commission of Fifteen Percent (15%) upon the gross proceeds received by the author on the first book, screenplay, or any other major work produced as a result of the consultation provided above.

(b) Second Book: A Ten Percent (10%) commission upon the gross proceeds received by the author of his or her second book, screenplay, or any other major work.

The only other fees for which the author will be responsible are those which cover out-of-pocket expenses in regard to presentation of the author's work to literary agents and/or publishers. Any copyediting and/or out-of-pocket expenses, which exceed twenty ($20.00) dollars shall require the prior approval of the author.

If the author changes his or her mind and chooses not to submit his or her work for publication or fails to consistently follow the guidance of Mr. Bird and, thus, does not complete his or her works, Mr. Bird will immediately be due the total amount of his regular fee.

C. Other

If the author chooses to continue to consult with Mr. Bird after the conclusion of the consultation period set forth above, such further participation and consultation, both as to how and for how long, will be negotiated separately.

D. Default

All costs, attorneys' fees, and other expenses of enforcing this agreement shall be paid to the prevailing party by the losers, including collection fees and costs.

Acknowledged and agreed to by:

_____   _____
Author   Thomas J. Bird

_____   _____
Date   Date

Chapter Eleven: Essential Suggestions

You are now ready to live your AW purpose. The following exercises will see to that.

Giving Your LCM Space, Too

Your LCM will attempt to distract you from your connecting through your CCM to your AW by posing many a concern.

To counter any negative effects from this, all that is needed is a space reserved for the LCM to initially voice its concerns so that these concerns don't become a distraction.

To do this, simply create a loosely drawn, one-inch, right-hand column on the side of each

"The best way out is always through."
ROBERT FROST

one of your writing surfaces. Whenever a thought pops up that is unrelated to what is being expressed through your connection, such as "Don't forget to pick up bananas at the market," simply toss it over into the space provided in the narrow column and keep going. This pattern will allow the LCM to express itself without interrupting the CCM connection with your AW.

"Beyond plants are animals, beyond animals is man, beyond man is the universe, the Big Light, let the Big Light in!"
JEAN TOOMER

Allow the relentless Creative Spirit, the Author Within, the Muse, your inner Truth and Wisdom to speak through you. Embrace everything that comes up. It's all part of the soul's experience in fulfilling its purpose. Allow and embrace everything as either your guide and ally or your teacher who seeks to show you how and when to follow your Spirit. Dare to be loved and empowered.
FRANCES
Student, Florida

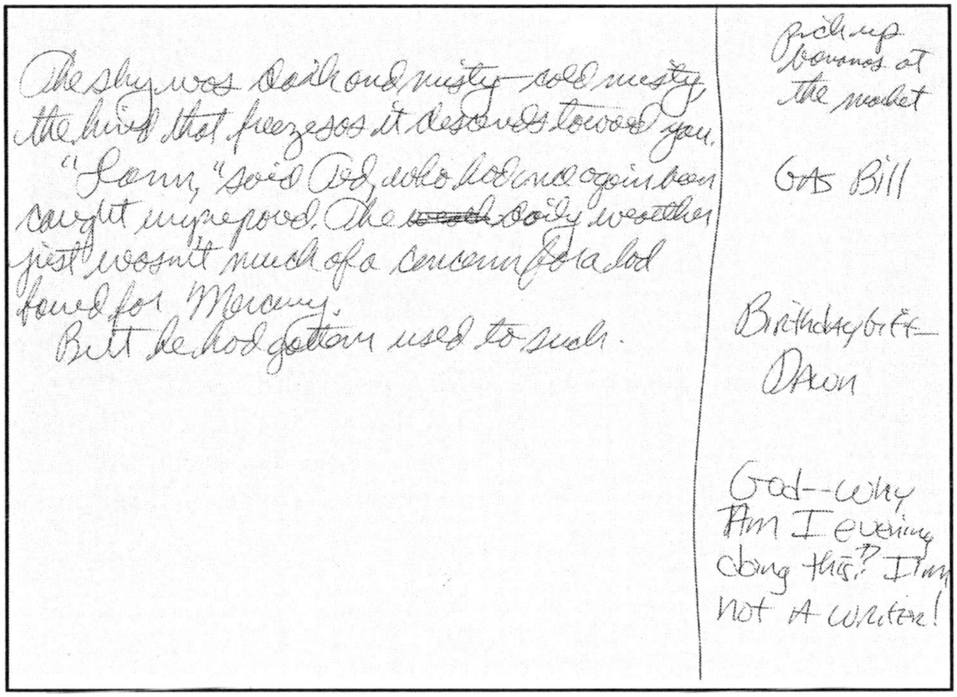

Sample poster board showing notes in the margins.

I AM THANKFULS

Step 1. Take the necessary steps to place yourself in your AW/CCM-connected state, insuring that some of your newly purchased writing surfaces are within arm's length.

Step 2. After achieving your necessary AW/CCM-connected state, write on your chosen writing surface the words "I am thankful" and then allow yourself to freely associate a response. Then, write the words "I am thankful" again and formulate a second response. Continue to do this as fast as possible until you have completely filled up one of your writing surfaces.

"Gratitude is not only the greatest of virtues, but the parent of all the others."

CICERO

"It was a struggle to sign up for your workshop (my husband and I are both currently unemployed), but I followed my gut instinct and went for it! Tom, it was worth every dollar to me, more than you could imagine. Thank you again for your help!"

INGRID
Student, Florida

NO REVIEW, JUST RELEASE

When you follow the inappropriate advice of your LCM, your essential connection with your CCM, the AW, and its voice, is stifled.

Thus it is important to avoid, at all costs, editing, reviewing, or looking for mistakes when you are in your CCM-connected state. As I will cover soon, there will be plenty of time for that later. But, anything other than releasing is to be avoided until much later. Simply allow your AW to express freely and openly in the space you have provided for it. If the LCM has anything to say, allow it to be said in the narrow, right-hand column you have created.

I WISH

Step 1. Slip into your AW-connected state, making sure that your chosen writing surface and new pens are nearby.

Step 2. Follow the same instructions for the last writing exercise. However, instead of directing your expression with the words "I am thankful," lead instead with the words "I wish." Fill at least one sheet of your chosen writing surface, or more if you would like.

GAPS

There are two specific reasons why you should just leave gaps in your rough work for any information or words or bits of information that you either don't know or don't remember.

First, you will continually sever the essential CCM connection with your AW each time you stop to research. As a result, nothing of any length or depth will ever be given the space and freedom that your AW needs. In the worst case scenario, of course, artist's block could surface.

Second, you can go back in and get the facts and figures you need to complete this stage later.

KEEP THE FLOW GOING BY ENDING IN THE MIDDLE AND WARMING UP BEFORE RESUMING

When we conclude a connected session at the end of an expression, or a section or chapter, it makes it very difficult and sometimes impossible to reinvigorate the same energy and flow when reconnecting with your CCM and then your AW for your next session.

To make it easiest for you to reconnect with where you were, how you felt, and what you were saying from a previous connected session, always conclude a session in the midst of expression. Then, all you will have to do the next session to reconnect is to enter into your AW-connected state and retrace the last few expressions you shared. The result will not only make it easy to maintain your flow and momentum from session to session, but will also offer your CCM connection a necessary seamlessness of expression.

JUST LET THE EXPRESSIONS AND FEELINGS FLY

The key to both releasing and maintaining your CCM connection with your AW comes from staying out of your LCM. Thus, when connected, by all means, just allow the expressions and feelings to fly out of you, which will enable you to stay within the necessary AW range of speed, insuring that you are remaining connected through your CCM.

DANCING AS FAST AS YOU CAN

While I was with the Pirates, we once had a young player who was a great athlete but far from being one of the brightest persons on the planet. Shortly after we had called him up from the minor leagues and added him to our roster, he was installed as a mainstay at third base. Defensively, third base, since it is so close to home plate, is a reactionary position. The ball comes at you so fast off the bat of a hitter that either you immediately know what to do with it, or you're maimed for life.

This young player had grown up in a baseball family. In fact, his father had been a famous big leaguer. So, he was very familiar with the game, which helped him perform marvelously at his position.

However, it wasn't too long after he arrived, that the club decided to move him over to shortstop. Shortstop is commonly referred to as "the thinking man's position," because from there a player can control the entire infield. It is also approximately twice the distance from home plate as third base. So, a player stationed at shortstop is often given much more time to ponder his or her move or reaction to a play.

This first year player, as mentioned, was a phenomenal third baseman. However, he was a terrible defensive shortstop. After one game in which he had committed several errors, he was asked by a well-meaning reporter why it was that he was such a good third baseman, but yet was not nearly as competent at his new position of shortstop.

A brighter player would have taken the question as an insult, but not this rookie, who responded immediately without any bias or negative reaction at all.

"Well, ya know," he began in his broken New Jersey accent, "when I was over at third base, you know, kinda like, when the ball was hit to me it got there real fast. But at shortstop, it bounces and bounces and bounces and takes a lot longer to get to me. In fact, it takes so long to get to me that I've got a lot of time to think about what it is that I am going to do with it when it finally gets there. And every time I think, I screw up."

"Every time I think, I screw up." How true, not only in baseball and with so much in life, but how especially appropriate with your connection. Thinking, of course, is a by-product of the LCM. Feeling is a by-product of your AW/CCM connection. Thus, when writing effectively, it is in your best interest to always be feeling and not thinking.

The best way to avoid involving yourself with the latter is to express as fast and as openly as you can. When you do so as fast as you can, you will stay within that AW-connected state, and there will be no room for the unnecessary interruptions, interferences, and input that comes through thinking.

This situation causes another significant dilemma, for our emotions, understanding, interpretations, and reactions grow as human beings every day. In the course of a few years, our viewpoint on many a major situation will have changed and altered substantially. These alterations in opinions and viewpoints will all be reflected in how your connection is eventually projected, leading to a massive inconsistency of voice and viewpoint, which will terribly skew whatever message your AW is attempting to release through your CCM.

Each life purpose represents one major idea, feeling, and/or expression. If the true meaning of your connection is skewed because of a consistently altering direction, the eventual result of what it is trying to release will be lost.

------------------ ⟲ ------------------

CHAPTER TWELVE: ALLOWING YOUR AW TO EXPRESS
YOUR PROJECT TO YOU

The very thought of creation brings forth a sort of panic, and it should. Because frankly, you do not by yourself have the ability to follow through on the project you feel called to complete. Thank God for our AWs. Because of our AWs, all we have to do is leave the expression up to them. Any approach other than that, of course, is completely counterproductive.

Okay, let's go over your checklist to make sure that you will have everything that you need for this grand and glorious journey on which you are just about to embark:

1. *By now you should have purchased the desired number of pens and the necessary number of sheets of your chosen writing surface.*

"You can convert your style into riches."
QUENTIN CRISP

2. *All of your contracts, especially the one meant to go to me, should have been sent out.*

3. *Your Living Outline should be posted and within clear view.*

4. *A weekly art schedule of no less than two hours a day, six days a week, should have been arranged.*

5. *Those in your life or with whom you share a home or office, or wherever it is that you write, should have been warned about the necessary private time that is needed for your art, and warned that you will enforce your rights in this regard at all costs.*

Here are the components of your art to keep in mind that will insure the successful completion of your project.

Read over the following list at least once every week, unless you run into a problem or a stoppage with your art. In the case of the latter, immediately turn to this page, read over the following to see which of the suggestions you have innocently forgotten or are in violation of, simply make whatever alterations are necessary in your approach, and you will be healed.

1. Always express as fast as you can.

2. Always precede any expression, or review of your art by first following the Three Rs of Writing.

3. "The cards" can be used not only for clearing, but they can be used for problem solv

"'On with the dance, let the joy be unconfined!' Is my motto, whether there's any dance to dance or any joy to unconfine."
MARK TWAIN

ing as well. So, if you ever feel confused and lost with any aspect of your art, all you have to do is to pull out some cards and just start brainstorming about how you feel. In no time at all your real problem will be brought to the surface, faced, understood, and taken care of so that you may continue on your way.

4. *Do not edit or review your work as you are expressing. Save all of that until the final steps outlined in the next chapter.*

5. *Leave gaps for any facts or bits of information that may pop up, but which you don't have at your disposal at the present time. Remember, there is no need to panic. Panic automatically shuts down an AW-connected state. All that needs to be researched will be covered in the activities outlined in the last step of the next chapter.*

6. *Take time to consistently reinforce each one of your successful sessions, no matter how large or small.*

7. *If any potentially distracting thoughts pop into your mind, dump them into your narrow right-hand column and get back to your art.*

8. *Work on your expression two hours a day, six days a week, no matter what happens. Don't judge your experience. Just stay within the lines of the program and all you ever wanted will pan out for you.*

"Some call it evolution and others call it God."
WILLIAM H. CARRUTH

9. *Make sure to never conclude a session at the end of a section.*

10. *Remember to just let the expressions fly out of you and onto the boards, allowing your AW to take you and your actions wherever you are both destined to go.*

11. *Don't review or study any other artist's work while going through this process for the first time.*

A FEW LAST-MINUTE REMINDERS

When beginning work on your project, please keep in mind:

➢ *The expression of any major project usually starts off slowly. Until you both get used to each other, don't allow any early sluggishness to rattle you. Just stay within the routine and in no time your art will have adjusted to you and you to it. When that happens, you both will begin operating as one and all will go a lot smoother.*

➢ *No matter how much preparatory work we have done up to this point, you will still not know exactly where it is that you are going from day to day. Remember, this is your AW's way of keeping you interested.*

➢ *Your project will end all on its own. You*

will also be given very little advance notice of when this will happen. About 45 minutes before it concludes is usually the norm. The reason for this short notice is so that your critical mind will not have time to come out and screw up your execution.

➤ *Remember that all you need to know, you already know, and all you need to have, you already have in your possession. To remind yourself of this fact, all you have to do at any time you choose is to look back through this book and at all that you have already accomplished.*

"He who hesitates is a damned fool."

MAE WEST

LET'S GO!

Okay, it's time to begin. I will get you started, but from this point forward it will be you and your AW expressing your project through your CCM. Of course, I will always be standing in the near background, smiling fondly.

Step 1. Get into your AW/CCM-connected state.

Step 2. Pull out a piece of your chosen writing surface, and in the center of it write a key word that best describes what it is you seek to express through your art.

Step 3. Allow yourself to completely free-associate any thoughts or feelings, whether they are directly tied to that which you will be expressing or not, by releasing them onto the lineless piece of paper before you.

Step 4. Once anything longer than a prepositional phrase on your character or theme pops out, immediately transfer your efforts to a second piece of paper and allow your project to begin expressing itself all on its own.

No matter how many days or weeks it takes, do not proceed on to the next chapter until your project has fully expressed itself. Go!

———— ❦ ————

CHAPTER THIRTEEN: ENHANCING

What is covered in this chapter should only be entered into after you have used this system to complete a full-length project.

When employing the following techniques, it is important to keep in mind that by following the suggestions made in this book that you have productively dealt with the vast majority of potential mistakes you could have made by limiting inappropriate LCM intervention. What this means is that no major overhaul of your material should be necessary. All that will be needed is covered in the following steps. Once you have finished using them, you are done and free to submit your work for sale, publication, distribution, or whatever.

"Where were you fellows when the paper was blank?"
FRED ALLEN

THE FIRST SWEEP THROUGH

On this sweep, we will be only focusing on major structural changes to your material. It is absolutely essential during this sweep, when you read over, revise, or enhance whatever it is that you have expressed, to make sure you are in an AW-connected state. Keep that in mind as you begin the following exercise, which will take several sessions to complete, to stay with the same schedule that you have utilized to complete the rough draft of your project. However, instead of composing your work during that time, devote your time to enhancing, and in no time at all your project will be fully revised, polished, and complete.

Repeat the following three steps each day until you have completely reviewed your draft and have noted any and all major changes you feel your work needs.

Step 1.   Enter into your AW-connected state.

Step 2.   Review your draft noting any and all major changes or alterations you would like to make to your work.

Major changes are defined as any alterations, rearrangements, subtractions, or additions that directly affect the general theme or direction of what you have already expressed. This does not include any changes of a more finite level, such as typos and grammatical changes. Remember, on this first sweep through, we are only concentrating on major structural enhancements. The easiest way that I have found to note these types of changes is to just

RICKY RICARDO: There you go again, wanting something that you haven't got.
LUCY RICARDO: I do not, I just want to see what I haven't got that I don't want.
                    I LOVE LUCY

write down any suggestions you may have on Post-It Notes and then place them on a bulletin board.

Step 3. Do not move on to the next step until you have fully completed this one.

"Resolve to know thyself; and know that he who finds himself, loses his misery."
MATTHEW ARNOLD

"It is a rare blessing to find a person who is willing to offer dreams come true and freedom to people – and who is deeply committed to supporting you in being who you really are. Tom is that and much more. He took me through an exercise that broke something free inside of me..."

KAREN
Student, Georgia

Changes that Heel Made On Lyrics

— Starts way to slow
— Skip first stanza
— Begin with last stanza
— Infact, turn the whole thing upside down
— Bigger break in consciousness between themes
— Then it should hit hard
— Let it hit hard
— Don't be so Afraid to show how you feel

Examples of art form changes.

Major Changes Heeded to Complete Painting

— More Red, more Red, More Red.
— Bring mysterious figure out of the shadows And sketch into the forefront
— much less darkness
— more light
— Alter grayness of clouds
— Sun shining onto figure standing in the Rain
— Much greener grass

Another example of art form changes.

THE SECOND SWEEP

This sweep is devoted to making the major changes you have noted. To do so, employ the following routine each time before you go to work with your material.

Step 1. Enter into your AW/CCM-connected state.

Step 2. Make whatever general changes you have proposed. It may take a few hours or several days to complete this task, if not weeks. In that case, simply follow these two steps each time you go into your art to make the necessary changes, rearrangements, or additions. Don't move on to the next step until you have fully completed this one.

"If you want a place in the sun you must leave the family tree."
OSAGE SAYING

POST-EXPRESSION RESEARCH

After you have completed making any and all necessary, general changes to your project, we can now turn to handling any postexpression research that needs to be attended to. Remember the gaps I told you to leave in your work that could be filled in with whatever information you did not have at the time? This is the time we gather whatever we need to fill in those gaps.

I know that you are tired of hearing this but, first of all, it is essential to insure that you are in your AW-connected state before you look back through your project.

214

To insure that you are in the necessary AW-connected state, begin devoting one-third of your allotted creative time each day to more work with the cards. Do not devote any more than one-third of your allotted time, though. Otherwise, you will become so obsessed with whatever it is that is coming out on the cards that it may cause you to neglect your other responsibilities.

As I am sure you are beginning to sense already, there is a very gentle and necessary balance that exists between the expression of new material and the revision of what you have already composed. You have gotten used to, maybe even become positively addicted to, the connected release of your AW through your CCM. You need it since it feeds you. This is where the positively addictive aspects of this connection, which I spoke about earlier, again comes into play. This connection not only feeds your life but the entire expressive experience and whatever goes along with it, including this phase of your revision.

What will come out at this time in your writing will most possibly be the beginning of your *Living Outline* for your next project.

Your AW, who doesn't want to confuse your LCM and, thus, cause you unnecessary pain or discomfort, would not initially offer you more than one idea at a time until you have fully completed a work. Or, on the other hand, you may have initially had a challenging time believing that you even had one project in you. You will be amazed at what comes out on the cards. Get used to it. Your life will continue to get more and more exciting as your AW is released.

"A heav'n on earth."
JOHN MILTON

215

All that you will learn through your connection with your AW will lead you to deeper conclusions and understandings about all areas of your life. These understandings will enable you to become a beacon of what is possible for all of us.

THE COLORS OF THE RAINBOW

This step and the three which follow are meant for the specific use of those whose art falls along literary lines. For the rest of you, feel free to conclude your work with your material by making any and all specific corrections or changes to your project that are necessary. Then, fast-forward to the section entitled *Sharing*. And keep moving forward with your next project.

After you move through your work with it on the cards, just follow the same steps you have already taken to get this far with your first project, and let number two come to life as well. During this final phase, you will find yourself feeling ambivalent. One part of you will be wildly excited to get your first project completed, while the other side of you will be feeling sad. This is normal. What you have expressed is like your child. There is a part of you that is anxious for your child to leave, while there is another portion that is terribly sad to have to say goodbye.

For those of you who have chosen writing as an art form, it is important for you to keep in mind that no one will ever know the purpose and meaning of your work better than you. With that

"An editor is one who separates the wheat from the chaff and prints the chaff."
ADLAI STEVENSON

216

in mind, for this step, you will be in charge of fine-tuning your words with the precision with which a grand piano is addressed. To do so, you will need one pack of four different colored highlighters. Since this step is one of a very conscious nature, it is essential that you continue to devote one-third of your writing time to your use of the cards.

If your efforts on your second work with the cards has taken you to the point where you can construct your *Living Outline* on your bulletin board, go ahead and do it. You will probably have noticed already that your work with the cards led you almost directly to the flushing out of your archetypes before moving quickly on to the outlining of your next work. This is normal for this stage of your development, since the vast majority, if not all, of your necessary cathartic clearing took place during your first interchange with the cards. If you have already moved past or do venture beyond the confines of your *Living Outline*, simply follow the exact same steps with your new project that you followed with your first and let 'er rip.

In regard to your highlighters, we will be using them to make six separate sweeps through your manuscript.

On the first pass-through, designate one highlighter for marking all of your *action verbs*.

On the second sweep, take another marker and highlight all of your *passive verbs*.

On the third pass-through, use the last two markers to highlight all of your *adjectives* and *adverbs*.

These three sweeps through your manuscript may take days, if not weeks, as will the

"I am earnest; I will not equivocate; I will not excuse; I will not retreat a single inch; I will be heard."

WILLIAM LLOYD
GARRISON

217

following steps. If you are confused and unsure on these different forms of language, this is a good time to go back and brush up on your grammar.

Once you have completed your highlighting, go through your manuscript and focus solely on each of your action verbs. With each and every action verb, ask yourself if you are using the most appropriate and expressive verb possible. If you have not done so, change whatever you have written to the appropriate verb.

After you have completed your work with the action verbs, then focus solely and completely upon your passive verbs. The liability with passive verbs is that they carry absolutely no imagery. So, they rob the reader of his or her ability to feel, hear, see, smell, or taste in reaction to your work.

Too many passive verbs, especially following in a row, will bore your reader or even possibly put him or her to sleep. Of course, you don't want to do that. So, when focusing upon your passive verbs, ask yourself, in each and every case, if there is a way you could possibly alter your sentences and/or paragraphs to rid your manuscript of so many passive verbs, and substitute action verbs in their place.

Verbs are the pulse of each one of your sentences. They direct, project forward, create, and release the most imagery. When they are perfectly attuned, not only will your words sing, but a substantial portion of your adjectives and adverbs will have become obsolete.

You now need to make one final pass-through to pluck out any adjectives and adverbs that are no longer needed, whose presence, if left

"He made righteousness readable."

JAMES BONE

218

untouched, may lead to your project being 'wordy.'

Once you have completed this step, which is designed to not only fine-tune your manuscript but to re-educate your LCM on the best way to allow the release of your AW, you are free to go on to the next phase.

"Unprovided with original learning, unformed in the habits of thinking, unskilled in the arts of composition, I resolved to write a book."
EDWARD GIBBON

Thank you for presenting the most exciting work-shop I have ever attended! Robert Frost said, "I am not a teacher, but an awakener." Indeed, you are an awakener!
SHERRY
Student, Arizona

219

This example shows sentences rearranged, verbs changed,
and adjectives and adverbs crossed out.

THE PIANIST IN US ALL

For those who have chosen to use the techniques in this book for the release of their writing, this step signals the typing of your manuscript into your computer. For this, you will need an easel or some sort of structure that will enable your chosen writing surfaces to be held at eye level.

There are a few responsibilities to keep in mind when performing this step.

First, continue to devote one-third of your designated writing time to working with your next project.

Second, make sure that you are in as relaxed a state as possible when you are typing. If you want to sip on some type of soothing beverage or play some relaxing music, now is the time to do so.

Being relaxed during this phase is essential. Being relaxed insures that you are as sensitive as possible to the flow of your material. By being as relaxed as possible, your heightened sensitivity will enable you to first sense and then smooth out any and all disjointed aspects of your text, which will have been caused by rearranging, adding, subtracting, or making general adjustments to your material.

Because of the tasks that still need to be completed in this phase, it is important that you personally input your material into your computer. If you are not a good typist, it may be time to consider buffing up on your typing skills. Or you can always utilize any one of a number of programs that enable you to speak your material into your computer. The one I recommend is

"Every situation – nay, every moment – is of infinite worth; for it is the representative of a whole eternity."

GOETHE

Dragon Speak Premier, which is available at just about any major office supply store or computer software supply.

When performing this step, I envision myself as a concert pianist who becomes at one with the music that is coming through me. In that way, I can feel the rhythm of my writing and make any necessary alterations to it.

When you have finished entering your manuscript into the computer, go on to the next step.

LET YOUR COMPUTER GO TO WORK FOR YOU

Now is the time to let your computer go to work for you. Once your manuscript has been typed into your computer, run it through your spell check and correct any misspellings.

I am not an advocate of computerized grammar checkers. You may feel differently. If so, run your manuscript through your grammar checker as well.

Once you have run it through your spell check, and possibly through your grammar checker, print out a hard copy of your manuscript.

ONE FINAL READTHROUGH

You should be continuing to work with your second project as you enter this final phase in the completion of your initial project. If you have

"There are hazards in anything one does, but there are greater hazards in doing nothing."
SHIRLEY WILLIAMS

222

fallen off on your commitment to your second work, get back to it. You should still be devoting a minimum of one-third of your allotted writing time to it each day.

As you read over your manuscript one last time, it is important to check for any necessary, flow-based adjustments which may be needed.

It is also essential to keep in mind that this literary child you have released will be with you always. No matter where the two of you choose to venture from this point forward, the connection, love, and interchange that has been shared will always be a part of you.

Finish reading through your manuscript one final time and then move on to the next step.

SHARING

I totally disagree that an artist's success should be determined by whether or not a work gets sold, distributed, or published.

I simply do not believe that you have to sell your work to be successful. I believe that the most valuable benefits of art come as the result of the AW/CCM connection itself. The joy, understanding, acceptance, and wisdom that come to you through connecting with your AW is unparalleled by any financial wealth or notoriety that you could possibly acquire.

However, if the sale of your material, which I see as the 'sharing' of your artistic wealth, is something that your AW is calling you to do, then by all means pursue it. For the essence of art is sharing. First, your AW shares with your

"If wisdom were offered me with the proviso that I should keep it shut up and refrain from declaring it, I should refuse. There's no delight in owning anything unshared."
SENECA
First Century, A.D.

223

"A man with God is always in the majority."

JOHN KNOX

CCM. A work manifests as a result. If you feel so called, you can share that work with others through distribution and sales. That is just how I choose to view this scenario. If you are a writer and seek a proven method to share your material through publication, I strongly recommend my book, *Spirited Publishing*.

If you do not feel called to share your work with anyone other than yourself, though, then whatever it is that you have expressed was meant for you and you alone.

Either way, though, you will have succeeded in doing what so many aspire to do, yet so few accomplish.

WHERE TO GO NOW

Where to go now? On to your next project of course! You are an artist. You will always be an artist. This is just who you are and what you do. By being who you are and doing what it is that you were meant to do, you will be a beacon of light for us all, a candle which will ignite many, if not tens of thousands, or millions, of other wicks. All of this comes as the result of just being you.

God, isn't life grand!

———— ✥ ————

JOURNAL

Time I scheduled to meet with my AW:

Time we actually met:

Our goal for today:

What we actually accomplished today:

Reinforcement I planned to offer myself for a job well done:

Reinforcement that I gave myself:

Other observations and notes:

My goal for my next session:

When we will meet again:

What I will use to reinforce my positive actions after the next session:

Time I scheduled to meet with my AW:

Time we actually met:

Our goal for today:

What we actually accomplished today:

Reinforcement I planned to offer myself for a job well done:

Reinforcement that I gave myself:

Other observations and notes:

My goal for my next session:

When we will meet again:

What I will use to reinforce my positive actions after the next session:

Time I scheduled to meet with my AW:

Time we actually met:

Our goal for today:

What we actually accomplished today:

Reinforcement I planned to offer myself for a job well done:

Reinforcement that I gave myself:

Other observations and notes:

My goal for my next session:

When we will meet again:

What I will use to reinforce my positive actions after the next session:

Time I scheduled to meet with my AW:

Time we actually met:

Our goal for today:

What we actually accomplished today:

Reinforcement I planned to offer myself for a job well done:

Reinforcement that I gave myself:

Other observations and notes:

My goal for my next session:

When we will meet again:

What I will use to reinforce my positive actions after the next session:

Time I scheduled to meet with my AW:

Time we actually met:

Our goal for today:

What we actually accomplished today:

Reinforcement I planned to offer myself for a job well done:

Reinforcement that I gave myself:

Other observations and notes:

My goal for my next session:

When we will meet again:

What I will use to reinforce my positive actions after the next session:

Time I scheduled to meet with my AW:

Time we actually met:

Our goal for today:

What we actually accomplished today:

Reinforcement I planned to offer myself for a job well done:

Reinforcement that I gave myself:

Other observations and notes:

My goal for my next session:

When we will meet again:

What I will use to reinforce my positive actions after the next session:

Time I scheduled to meet with my AW:

Time we actually met:

Our goal for today:

What we actually accomplished today:

Reinforcement I planned to offer myself for a job well done:

Reinforcement that I gave myself:

Other observations and notes:

My goal for my next session:

When we will meet again:

What I will use to reinforce my positive actions after the next session:

Time I scheduled to meet with my AW:

Time we actually met:

Our goal for today:

What we actually accomplished today:

Reinforcement I planned to offer myself for a job well done:

Reinforcement that I gave myself:

Other observations and notes:

My goal for my next session:

When we will meet again:

What I will use to reinforce my positive actions after the next session:

YOUR ARTIST WITHIN

Day:

Time I scheduled to meet with my AW:

Time we actually met:

Our goal for today:

What we actually accomplished today:

Reinforcement I planned to offer myself for a job well done:

Reinforcement that I gave myself:

Other observations and notes:

My goal for my next session:

When we will meet again:

What I will use to reinforce my positive actions after the next session:

Time I scheduled to meet with my AW:

Time we actually met:

Our goal for today:

What we actually accomplished today:

Reinforcement I planned to offer myself for a job well done:

Reinforcement that I gave myself:

Other observations and notes:

My goal for my next session:

When we will meet again:

What I will use to reinforce my positive actions after the next session:

Time I scheduled to meet with my AW:

Time we actually met:

Our goal for today:

What we actually accomplished today:

Reinforcement I planned to offer myself for a job well done:

Reinforcement that I gave myself:

Other observations and notes:

My goal for my next session:

When we will meet again:

What I will use to reinforce my positive actions after the next session:

Time I scheduled to meet with my AW:

Time we actually met:

Our goal for today:

What we actually accomplished today:

Reinforcement I planned to offer myself for a job well done:

Reinforcement that I gave myself:

Other observations and notes:

My goal for my next session:

When we will meet again:

What I will use to reinforce my positive actions after the next session:

Time I scheduled to meet with my AW:

Time we actually met:

Our goal for today:

What we actually accomplished today:

Reinforcement I planned to offer myself for a job well done:

Reinforcement that I gave myself:

Other observations and notes:

My goal for my next session:

When we will meet again:

What I will use to reinforce my positive actions after the next session:

Time I scheduled to meet with my AW:

Time we actually met:

Our goal for today:

What we actually accomplished today:

Reinforcement I planned to offer myself for a job well done:

Reinforcement that I gave myself:

Other observations and notes:

My goal for my next session:

When we will meet again:

What I will use to reinforce my positive actions after the next session:

Time I scheduled to meet with my AW:

Time we actually met:

Our goal for today:

What we actually accomplished today:

Reinforcement I planned to offer myself for a job well done:

Reinforcement that I gave myself:

Other observations and notes:

My goal for my next session:

When we will meet again:

What I will use to reinforce my positive actions after the next session:

Time I scheduled to meet with my AW:

Time we actually met:

Our goal for today:

What we actually accomplished today:

Reinforcement I planned to offer myself for a job well done:

Reinforcement that I gave myself:

Other observations and notes:

My goal for my next session:

When we will meet again:

What I will use to reinforce my positive actions after the next session:

Time I scheduled to meet with my AW:

Time we actually met:

Our goal for today:

What we actually accomplished today:

Reinforcement I planned to offer myself for a job well done:

Reinforcement that I gave myself:

Other observations and notes:

My goal for my next session:

When we will meet again:

What I will use to reinforce my positive actions after the next session:

Time I scheduled to meet with my AW:

Time we actually met:

Our goal for today:

What we actually accomplished today:

Reinforcement I planned to offer myself for a job well done:

Reinforcement that I gave myself:

Other observations and notes:

My goal for my next session:

When we will meet again:

What I will use to reinforce my positive actions after the next session:

Time I scheduled to meet with my AW:

Time we actually met:

Our goal for today:

What we actually accomplished today:

Reinforcement I planned to offer myself for a job well done:

Reinforcement that I gave myself:

Other observations and notes:

My goal for my next session:

When we will meet again:

What I will use to reinforce my positive actions after the next session:

Time I scheduled to meet with my AW:

Time we actually met:

Our goal for today:

What we actually accomplished today:

Reinforcement I planned to offer myself for a job well done:

Reinforcement that I gave myself:

Other observations and notes:

My goal for my next session:

When we will meet again:

What I will use to reinforce my positive actions after the next session:

Time I scheduled to meet with my AW:

Time we actually met:

Our goal for today:

What we actually accomplished today:

Reinforcement I planned to offer myself for a job well done:

Reinforcement that I gave myself:

Other observations and notes:

My goal for my next session:

When we will meet again:

What I will use to reinforce my positive actions after the next session:

Time I scheduled to meet with my AW:

Time we actually met:

Our goal for today:

What we actually accomplished today:

Reinforcement I planned to offer myself for a job well done:

Reinforcement that I gave myself:

Other observations and notes:

My goal for my next session:

When we will meet again:

What I will use to reinforce my positive actions after the next session:

Time I scheduled to meet with my AW:

Time we actually met:

Our goal for today:

What we actually accomplished today:

Reinforcement I planned to offer myself for a job well done:

Reinforcement that I gave myself:

Other observations and notes:

My goal for my next session:

When we will meet again:

What I will use to reinforce my positive actions after the next session:

Time I scheduled to meet with my AW:

Time we actually met:

Our goal for today:

What we actually accomplished today:

Reinforcement I planned to offer myself for a job well done:

Reinforcement that I gave myself:

Other observations and notes:

My goal for my next session:

When we will meet again:

What I will use to reinforce my positive actions after the next session:

Time I scheduled to meet with my AW:

Time we actually met:

Our goal for today:

What we actually accomplished today:

Reinforcement I planned to offer myself for a job well done:

Reinforcement that I gave myself:

Other observations and notes:

My goal for my next session:

When we will meet again:

What I will use to reinforce my positive actions after the next session:

Time I scheduled to meet with my AW:

Time we actually met:

Our goal for today:

What we actually accomplished today:

Reinforcement I planned to offer myself for a job well done:

Reinforcement that I gave myself:

Other observations and notes:

My goal for my next session:

When we will meet again:

What I will use to reinforce my positive actions after the next session:

Time I scheduled to meet with my AW:

Time we actually met:

Our goal for today:

What we actually accomplished today:

Reinforcement I planned to offer myself for a job well done:

Reinforcement that I gave myself:

Other observations and notes:

My goal for my next session:

When we will meet again:

What I will use to reinforce my positive actions after the next session:

Time I scheduled to meet with my AW:

Time we actually met:

Our goal for today:

What we actually accomplished today:

Reinforcement I planned to offer myself for a job well done:

Reinforcement that I gave myself:

Other observations and notes:

My goal for my next session:

When we will meet again:

What I will use to reinforce my positive actions after the next session:

Time I scheduled to meet with my AW:

Time we actually met:

Our goal for today:

What we actually accomplished today:

Reinforcement I planned to offer myself for a job well done:

Reinforcement that I gave myself:

Other observations and notes:

My goal for my next session:

When we will meet again:

What I will use to reinforce my positive actions after the next session:

Time I scheduled to meet with my AW:

Time we actually met:

Our goal for today:

What we actually accomplished today:

Reinforcement I planned to offer myself for a job well done:

Reinforcement that I gave myself:

Other observations and notes:

My goal for my next session:

When we will meet again:

What I will use to reinforce my positive actions after the next session:

Time I scheduled to meet with my AW:

Time we actually met:

Our goal for today:

What we actually accomplished today:

Reinforcement I planned to offer myself for a job well done:

Reinforcement that I gave myself:

Other observations and notes:

My goal for my next session:

When we will meet again:

What I will use to reinforce my positive actions after the next session:

Time I scheduled to meet with my AW:

Time we actually met:

Our goal for today:

What we actually accomplished today:

Reinforcement I planned to offer myself for a job well done:

Reinforcement that I gave myself:

Other observations and notes:

My goal for my next session:

When we will meet again:

What I will use to reinforce my positive actions after the next session:

Time I scheduled to meet with my AW:

Time we actually met:

Our goal for today:

What we actually accomplished today:

Reinforcement I planned to offer myself for a job well done:

Reinforcement that I gave myself:

Other observations and notes:

My goal for my next session:

When we will meet again:

What I will use to reinforce my positive actions after the next session:

Time I scheduled to meet with my AW:

Time we actually met:

Our goal for today:

What we actually accomplished today:

Reinforcement I planned to offer myself for a job well done:

Reinforcement that I gave myself:

Other observations and notes:

My goal for my next session:

When we will meet again:

What I will use to reinforce my positive actions after the next session:

Time I scheduled to meet with my AW:

Time we actually met:

Our goal for today:

What we actually accomplished today:

Reinforcement I planned to offer myself for a job well done:

Reinforcement that I gave myself:

Other observations and notes:

My goal for my next session:

When we will meet again:

What I will use to reinforce my positive actions after the next session:

Time I scheduled to meet with my AW:

Time we actually met:

Our goal for today:

What we actually accomplished today:

Reinforcement I planned to offer myself for a job well done:

Reinforcement that I gave myself:

Other observations and notes:

My goal for my next session:

When we will meet again:

What I will use to reinforce my positive actions after the next session:

Time I scheduled to meet with my AW:

Time we actually met:

Our goal for today:

What we actually accomplished today:

Reinforcement I planned to offer myself for a job well done:

Reinforcement that I gave myself:

Other observations and notes:

My goal for my next session:

When we will meet again:

What I will use to reinforce my positive actions after the next session:

Time I scheduled to meet with my AW:

Time we actually met:

Our goal for today:

What we actually accomplished today:

Reinforcement I planned to offer myself for a job well done:

Reinforcement that I gave myself:

Other observations and notes:

My goal for my next session:

When we will meet again:

What I will use to reinforce my positive actions after the next session:

Time I scheduled to meet with my AW:

Time we actually met:

Our goal for today:

What we actually accomplished today:

Reinforcement I planned to offer myself for a job well done:

Reinforcement that I gave myself:

Other observations and notes:

My goal for my next session:

When we will meet again:

What I will use to reinforce my positive actions after the next session:

Time I scheduled to meet with my AW:

Time we actually met:

Our goal for today:

What we actually accomplished today:

Reinforcement I planned to offer myself for a job well done:

Reinforcement that I gave myself:

Other observations and notes:

My goal for my next session:

When we will meet again:

What I will use to reinforce my positive actions after the next session:

Time I scheduled to meet with my AW:

Time we actually met:

Our goal for today:

What we actually accomplished today:

Reinforcement I planned to offer myself for a job well done:

Reinforcement that I gave myself:

Other observations and notes:

My goal for my next session:

When we will meet again:

What I will use to reinforce my positive actions after the next session:

Time I scheduled to meet with my AW:

Time we actually met:

Our goal for today:

What we actually accomplished today:

Reinforcement I planned to offer myself for a job well done:

Reinforcement that I gave myself:

Other observations and notes:

My goal for my next session:

When we will meet again:

What I will use to reinforce my positive actions after the next session:

Time I scheduled to meet with my AW:

Time we actually met:

Our goal for today:

What we actually accomplished today:

Reinforcement I planned to offer myself for a job well done:

Reinforcement that I gave myself:

Other observations and notes:

My goal for my next session:

When we will meet again:

What I will use to reinforce my positive actions after the next session:

Time I scheduled to meet with my AW:

Time we actually met:

Our goal for today:

What we actually accomplished today:

Reinforcement I planned to offer myself for a job well done:

Reinforcement that I gave myself:

Other observations and notes:

My goal for my next session:

When we will meet again:

What I will use to reinforce my positive actions after the next session:

Time I scheduled to meet with my AW:

Time we actually met:

Our goal for today:

What we actually accomplished today:

Reinforcement I planned to offer myself for a job well done:

Reinforcement that I gave myself:

Other observations and notes:

My goal for my next session:

When we will meet again:

What I will use to reinforce my positive actions after the next session:

Time I scheduled to meet with my AW:

Time we actually met:

Our goal for today:

What we actually accomplished today:

Reinforcement I planned to offer myself for a job well done:

Reinforcement that I gave myself:

Other observations and notes:

My goal for my next session:

When we will meet again:

What I will use to reinforce my positive actions after the next session:

Time I scheduled to meet with my AW:

Time we actually met:

Our goal for today:

What we actually accomplished today:

Reinforcement I planned to offer myself for a job well done:

Reinforcement that I gave myself:

Other observations and notes:

My goal for my next session:

When we will meet again:

What I will use to reinforce my positive actions after the next session:

Time I scheduled to meet with my AW:

Time we actually met:

Our goal for today:

What we actually accomplished today:

Reinforcement I planned to offer myself for a job well done:

Reinforcement that I gave myself:

Other observations and notes:

My goal for my next session:

When we will meet again:

What I will use to reinforce my positive actions after the next session:

Time I scheduled to meet with my AW:

Time we actually met:

Our goal for today:

What we actually accomplished today:

Reinforcement I planned to offer myself for a job well done:

Reinforcement that I gave myself:

Other observations and notes:

My goal for my next session:

When we will meet again:

What I will use to reinforce my positive actions after the next session:

Time I scheduled to meet with my AW:

Time we actually met:

Our goal for today:

What we actually accomplished today:

Reinforcement I planned to offer myself for a job well done:

Reinforcement that I gave myself:

Other observations and notes:

My goal for my next session:

When we will meet again:

What I will use to reinforce my positive actions after the next session:

Time I scheduled to meet with my AW:

Time we actually met:

Our goal for today:

What we actually accomplished today:

Reinforcement I planned to offer myself for a job well done:

Reinforcement that I gave myself:

Other observations and notes:

My goal for my next session:

When we will meet again:

What I will use to reinforce my positive actions after the next session:

Time I scheduled to meet with my AW:

Time we actually met:

Our goal for today:

What we actually accomplished today:

Reinforcement I planned to offer myself for a job well done:

Reinforcement that I gave myself:

Other observations and notes:

My goal for my next session:

When we will meet again:

What I will use to reinforce my positive actions after the next session:

Time I scheduled to meet with my AW:

Time we actually met:

Our goal for today:

What we actually accomplished today:

Reinforcement I planned to offer myself for a job well done:

Reinforcement that I gave myself:

Other observations and notes:

My goal for my next session:

When we will meet again:

What I will use to reinforce my positive actions after the next session:

Time I scheduled to meet with my AW:

Time we actually met:

Our goal for today:

What we actually accomplished today:

Reinforcement I planned to offer myself for a job well done:

Reinforcement that I gave myself:

Other observations and notes:

My goal for my next session:

When we will meet again:

What I will use to reinforce my positive actions after the next session:

Time I scheduled to meet with my AW:

Time we actually met:

Our goal for today:

What we actually accomplished today:

Reinforcement I planned to offer myself for a job well done:

Reinforcement that I gave myself:

Other observations and notes:

My goal for my next session:

When we will meet again:

What I will use to reinforce my positive actions after the next session:

Time I scheduled to meet with my AW:

Time we actually met:

Our goal for today:

What we actually accomplished today:

Reinforcement I planned to offer myself for a job well done:

Reinforcement that I gave myself:

Other observations and notes:

My goal for my next session:

When we will meet again:

What I will use to reinforce my positive actions after the next session:

Time I scheduled to meet with my AW:

Time we actually met:

Our goal for today:

What we actually accomplished today:

Reinforcement I planned to offer myself for a job well done:

Reinforcement that I gave myself:

Other observations and notes:

My goal for my next session:

When we will meet again:

What I will use to reinforce my positive actions after the next session:

Time I scheduled to meet with my AW:

Time we actually met:

Our goal for today:

What we actually accomplished today:

Reinforcement I planned to offer myself for a job well done:

Reinforcement that I gave myself:

Other observations and notes:

My goal for my next session:

When we will meet again:

What I will use to reinforce my positive actions after the next session:

Time I scheduled to meet with my AW:

Time we actually met:

Our goal for today:

What we actually accomplished today:

Reinforcement I planned to offer myself for a job well done:

Reinforcement that I gave myself:

Other observations and notes:

My goal for my next session:

When we will meet again:

What I will use to reinforce my positive actions after the next session:

Time I scheduled to meet with my AW:

Time we actually met:

Our goal for today:

What we actually accomplished today:

Reinforcement I planned to offer myself for a job well done:

Reinforcement that I gave myself:

Other observations and notes:

My goal for my next session:

When we will meet again:

What I will use to reinforce my positive actions after the next session:

Time I scheduled to meet with my AW:

Time we actually met:

Our goal for today:

What we actually accomplished today:

Reinforcement I planned to offer myself for a job well done:

Reinforcement that I gave myself:

Other observations and notes:

My goal for my next session:

When we will meet again:

What I will use to reinforce my positive actions after the next session:

Time I scheduled to meet with my AW:

Time we actually met:

Our goal for today:

What we actually accomplished today:

Reinforcement I planned to offer myself for a job well done:

Reinforcement that I gave myself:

Other observations and notes:

My goal for my next session:

When we will meet again:

What I will use to reinforce my positive actions after the next session:

Time I scheduled to meet with my AW:

Time we actually met:

Our goal for today:

What we actually accomplished today:

Reinforcement I planned to offer myself for a job well done:

Reinforcement that I gave myself:

Other observations and notes:

My goal for my next session:

When we will meet again:

What I will use to reinforce my positive actions after the next session:

Time I scheduled to meet with my AW:

Time we actually met:

Our goal for today:

What we actually accomplished today:

Reinforcement I planned to offer myself for a job well done:

Reinforcement that I gave myself:

Other observations and notes:

My goal for my next session:

When we will meet again:

What I will use to reinforce my positive actions after the next session:

Time I scheduled to meet with my AW:

Time we actually met:

Our goal for today:

What we actually accomplished today:

Reinforcement I planned to offer myself for a job well done:

Reinforcement that I gave myself:

Other observations and notes:

My goal for my next session:

When we will meet again:

What I will use to reinforce my positive actions after the next session:

Time I scheduled to meet with my AW:

Time we actually met:

Our goal for today:

What we actually accomplished today:

Reinforcement I planned to offer myself for a job well done:

Reinforcement that I gave myself:

Other observations and notes:

My goal for my next session:

When we will meet again:

What I will use to reinforce my positive actions after the next session:

Time I scheduled to meet with my AW:

Time we actually met:

Our goal for today:

What we actually accomplished today:

Reinforcement I planned to offer myself for a job well done:

Reinforcement that I gave myself:

Other observations and notes:

My goal for my next session:

When we will meet again:

What I will use to reinforce my positive actions after the next session:

Time I scheduled to meet with my AW:

Time we actually met:

Our goal for today:

What we actually accomplished today:

Reinforcement I planned to offer myself for a job well done:

Reinforcement that I gave myself:

Other observations and notes:

My goal for my next session:

When we will meet again:

What I will use to reinforce my positive actions after the next session:

Time I scheduled to meet with my AW:

Time we actually met:

Our goal for today:

What we actually accomplished today:

Reinforcement I planned to offer myself for a job well done:

Reinforcement that I gave myself:

Other observations and notes:

My goal for my next session:

When we will meet again:

What I will use to reinforce my positive actions after the next session:

Time I scheduled to meet with my AW:

Time we actually met:

Our goal for today:

What we actually accomplished today:

Reinforcement I planned to offer myself for a job well done:

Reinforcement that I gave myself:

Other observations and notes:

My goal for my next session:

When we will meet again:

What I will use to reinforce my positive actions after the next session:

Time I scheduled to meet with my AW:

Time we actually met:

Our goal for today:

What we actually accomplished today:

Reinforcement I planned to offer myself for a job well done:

Reinforcement that I gave myself:

Other observations and notes:

My goal for my next session:

When we will meet again:

What I will use to reinforce my positive actions after the next session:

Time I scheduled to meet with my AW:

Time we actually met:

Our goal for today:

What we actually accomplished today:

Reinforcement I planned to offer myself for a job well done:

Reinforcement that I gave myself:

Other observations and notes:

My goal for my next session:

When we will meet again:

What I will use to reinforce my positive actions after the next session:

Time I scheduled to meet with my AW:

Time we actually met:

Our goal for today:

What we actually accomplished today:

Reinforcement I planned to offer myself for a job well done:

Reinforcement that I gave myself:

Other observations and notes:

My goal for my next session:

When we will meet again:

What I will use to reinforce my positive actions after the next session:

Time I scheduled to meet with my AW:

Time we actually met:

Our goal for today:

What we actually accomplished today:

Reinforcement I planned to offer myself for a job well done:

Reinforcement that I gave myself:

Other observations and notes:

My goal for my next session:

When we will meet again:

What I will use to reinforce my positive actions after the next session:

Time I scheduled to meet with my AW:

Time we actually met:

Our goal for today:

What we actually accomplished today:

Reinforcement I planned to offer myself for a job well done:

Reinforcement that I gave myself:

Other observations and notes:

My goal for my next session:

When we will meet again:

What I will use to reinforce my positive actions after the next session:

Time I scheduled to meet with my AW:

Time we actually met:

Our goal for today:

What we actually accomplished today:

Reinforcement I planned to offer myself for a job well done:

Reinforcement that I gave myself:

Other observations and notes:

My goal for my next session:

When we will meet again:

What I will use to reinforce my positive actions after the next session:

Time I scheduled to meet with my AW:

Time we actually met:

Our goal for today:

What we actually accomplished today:

Reinforcement I planned to offer myself for a job well done:

Reinforcement that I gave myself:

Other observations and notes:

My goal for my next session:

When we will meet again:

What I will use to reinforce my positive actions after the next session:

Time I scheduled to meet with my AW:

Time we actually met:

Our goal for today:

What we actually accomplished today:

Reinforcement I planned to offer myself for a job well done:

Reinforcement that I gave myself:

Other observations and notes:

My goal for my next session:

When we will meet again:

What I will use to reinforce my positive actions after the next session:

Time I scheduled to meet with my AW:

Time we actually met:

Our goal for today:

What we actually accomplished today:

Reinforcement I planned to offer myself for a job well done:

Reinforcement that I gave myself:

Other observations and notes:

My goal for my next session:

When we will meet again:

What I will use to reinforce my positive actions after the next session:

Time I scheduled to meet with my AW:

Time we actually met:

Our goal for today:

What we actually accomplished today:

Reinforcement I planned to offer myself for a job well done:

Reinforcement that I gave myself:

Other observations and notes:

My goal for my next session:

When we will meet again:

What I will use to reinforce my positive actions after the next session:

Time I scheduled to meet with my AW:

Time we actually met:

Our goal for today:

What we actually accomplished today:

Reinforcement I planned to offer myself for a job well done:

Reinforcement that I gave myself:

Other observations and notes:

My goal for my next session:

When we will meet again:

What I will use to reinforce my positive actions after the next session:

Time I scheduled to meet with my AW:

Time we actually met:

Our goal for today:

What we actually accomplished today:

Reinforcement I planned to offer myself for a job well done:

Reinforcement that I gave myself:

Other observations and notes:

My goal for my next session:

When we will meet again:

What I will use to reinforce my positive actions after the next session:

Time I scheduled to meet with my AW:

Time we actually met:

Our goal for today:

What we actually accomplished today:

Reinforcement I planned to offer myself for a job well done:

Reinforcement that I gave myself:

Other observations and notes:

My goal for my next session:

When we will meet again:

What I will use to reinforce my positive actions after the next session:

Time I scheduled to meet with my AW:

Time we actually met:

Our goal for today:

What we actually accomplished today:

Reinforcement I planned to offer myself for a job well done:

Reinforcement that I gave myself:

Other observations and notes:

My goal for my next session:

When we will meet again:

What I will use to reinforce my positive actions after the next session:

Time I scheduled to meet with my AW:

Time we actually met:

Our goal for today:

What we actually accomplished today:

Reinforcement I planned to offer myself for a job well done:

Reinforcement that I gave myself:

Other observations and notes:

My goal for my next session:

When we will meet again:

What I will use to reinforce my positive actions after the next session:

Time I scheduled to meet with my AW:

Time we actually met:

Our goal for today:

What we actually accomplished today:

Reinforcement I planned to offer myself for a job well done:

Reinforcement that I gave myself:

Other observations and notes:

My goal for my next session:

When we will meet again:

What I will use to reinforce my positive actions after the next session:

Time I scheduled to meet with my AW:

Time we actually met:

Our goal for today:

What we actually accomplished today:

Reinforcement I planned to offer myself for a job well done:

Reinforcement that I gave myself:

Other observations and notes:

My goal for my next session:

When we will meet again:

What I will use to reinforce my positive actions after the next session:

Time I scheduled to meet with my AW:

Time we actually met:

Our goal for today:

What we actually accomplished today:

Reinforcement I planned to offer myself for a job well done:

Reinforcement that I gave myself:

Other observations and notes:

My goal for my next session:

When we will meet again:

What I will use to reinforce my positive actions after the next session:

Time I scheduled to meet with my AW:

Time we actually met:

Our goal for today:

What we actually accomplished today:

Reinforcement I planned to offer myself for a job well done:

Reinforcement that I gave myself:

Other observations and notes:

My goal for my next session:

When we will meet again:

What I will use to reinforce my positive actions after the next session:

Time I scheduled to meet with my AW:

Time we actually met:

Our goal for today:

What we actually accomplished today:

Reinforcement I planned to offer myself for a job well done:

Reinforcement that I gave myself:

Other observations and notes:

My goal for my next session:

When we will meet again:

What I will use to reinforce my positive actions after the next session:

Time I scheduled to meet with my AW:

Time we actually met:

Our goal for today:

What we actually accomplished today:

Reinforcement I planned to offer myself for a job well done:

Reinforcement that I gave myself:

Other observations and notes:

My goal for my next session:

When we will meet again:

What I will use to reinforce my positive actions after the next session:

BOOKS AND PROGRAMS OFFERED BY TOM BIRD
15% OFF When Ordering Through
www.YourArtistWithin.com

YOUR ARTIST WITHIN
This book shows you how to make the ultimate of all connections and to live your life's purpose. For the aspiring author, it also shares a system for completing a book in 45 days or less. Price $27.00 / **SALE $24.00**.

TOM BIRD'S 2004 SELECTIVE GUIDE TO LITERARY AGENTS DATABASE
The ultimate consumer's guide for the aspiring author looking to land the right literary agent. Newly updated, this year's edition boasts over 400 of the industry's top literary agents. Organized as a computer database, this unique version allows you to access your chosen sources with a click of your mouse and to merge them all together, saving you days of precious time when submitting query letters. (E-mailed to you after purchase.) Price $39.00 / **SALE $33.00.**

THE SPIRIT OF PUBLISHING: The Ultimate Guide for Getting Whatever It Is That You Write Into Print Now!
Recently revised and updated, this mainstay of Tom's teaching offers you absolutely everything that you will need to see your work in print, no matter what it is that you want to write. Plenty of winning examples given, including query letters and submission packages. Price $29.00 / **SALE $25.00.**

WE DO THE WORK FOR YOU
Tom will review your query letter once, then, after your approval, we'll e-mail the query for you. All the responses will come direct to you and your computer. Quick, simple, easy. Price $115.00 / **SALE $97.75.**

PURCHASE ALL THREE FOR EXTRA DISCOUNTS:
The Spirit of Publishing: How to Get Your Writing into Print Now!, Your Artist Within; and the Agent's Database, all for $82.00 / **SALE $74.00.**

Ordering Information: S&H $5.00 for 1-2 books, $6.00 for 3. Arizona Residents, please add 7% Sales Tax. Please make your checks out to: Tom Bird Seminars, Inc. and mail to, P. O. Box 4306, Sedona, AZ 86340. Or, fax Visa, MC, Discover, or AMX credit card information to 928/203-0264. Online Ordering is also available through PayPal.

For further information, feel free to either give us a call at 928/203-0265 or visit our website at http://www.YourArtistWithin.com

All Major Credit Cards Accepted.

(Prices subject to change without notice.)

Printed in the United States
21443LVS00002B/129-142